# KAETHE KOLLWITZ DRAWINGS

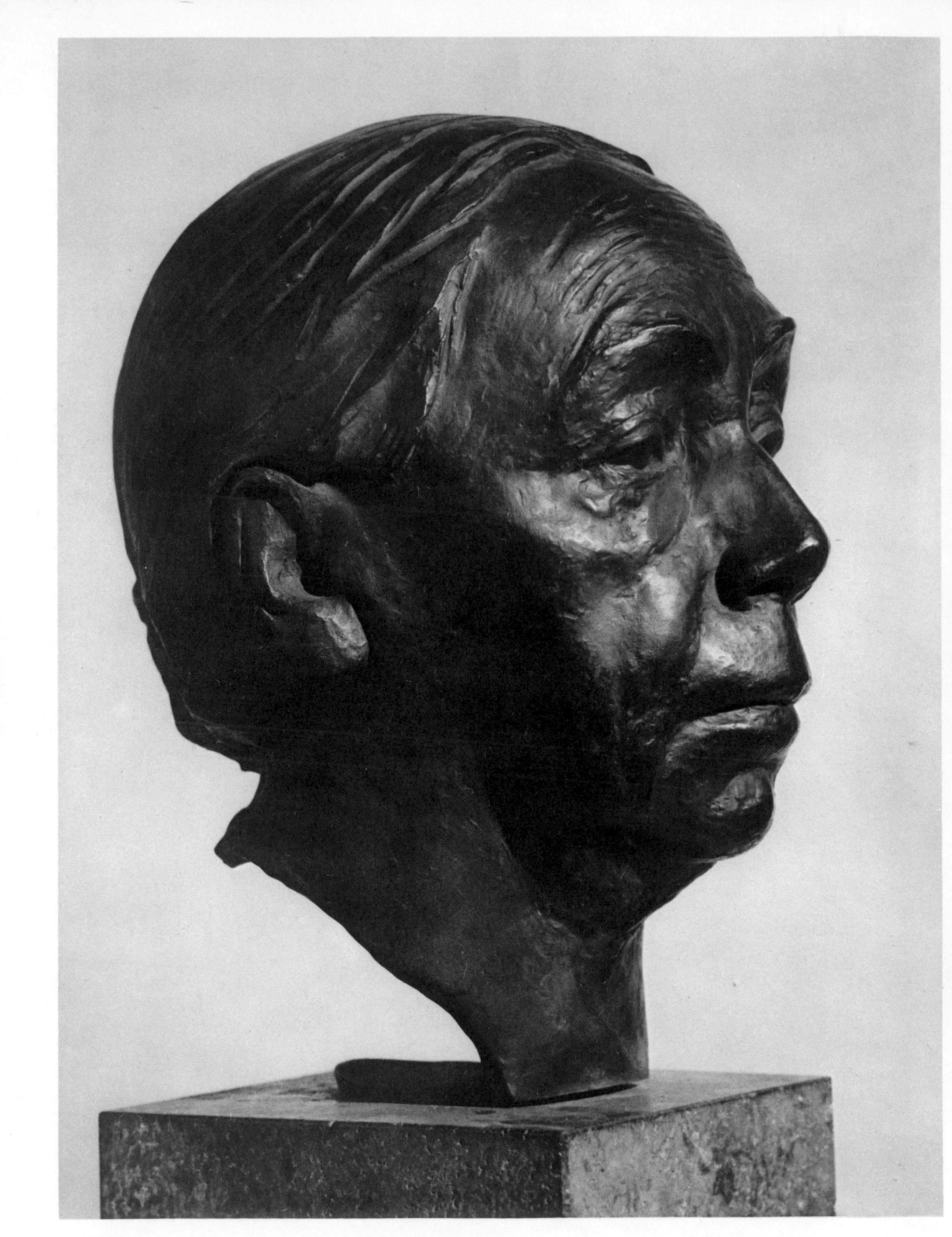

A Self Portrait

Herbert Bittner

# KAETHE KOLLWITZ

## DRAWINGS

THOMAS YOSELOFF
*NEW YORK* *LONDON*

Library of Congress Catalogue Card Number: 59-8230



THOMAS YOSELOFF, *Publisher*
11 EAST 36TH STREET
NEW YORK 16, N. Y.

THOMAS YOSELOFF LTD.
123 NEW BOND STREET
LONDON W. 1, ENGLAND

First printing August 1959
Second printing August 1962



Printed in the United States of America

TO

RUDOLF PIERRE WENDEL

His Family and His Friends

L'oeuvre de Kaethe Kollwitz
est le plus grand poème de l'Allemagne de ce temps,
que reflète l'épreuve et la peine
des humbles et simples.
Cette femme au coeur viril les a pris dans ses yeux,
dans ses bras maternels,
avec une sombre et tendre pitié.
Elle est la voix du silence des peuples sacrifiés.

Romain Rolland
1927

The work of Kaethe Kollwitz
which reflects the ordeal and the pain
of the humble and simple
is the grandest German poem of the age.
This woman of virile heart
has looked on them, has taken them into
her motherly arms,
with a solemn and tender compassion.
She is the voice of the silence of the sacrificed.

Romain Rolland
1927

*I believe that drawing is a good instrument in the fight against the present Middle Ages.*

GEORGE GROSZ, in a conversation with the author.

"I WAS OFTEN IN DESPAIR OVER THE UNSATISFACTORY RESULT WHEN A GOOD DRAWING was transferred to the copperplate," wrote Kaethe Kollwitz in 1921, in a letter to her first biographer, Arthur Bonus. Etchings, woodcuts, and even lithographs always retain traces of the raw material and handicraft. In drawings, the line of the pen, pencil, charcoal, crayon, or the brush stroke in sepia or wash, is freer and more valuable as the immediate precipitation of the artist's inner vision—*disegno interno* as Federigo Zuccari calls it—of his feeling and his temperament.

Zuccari and Vasari conceive of a drawing as more definite than just the almost spiritual *pensiero,* the *prima idea* or *disegno esterno.* Through corrections, the painters of the Renaissance approached—but only approached—a *disegno finito.* Form, power, and beauty—and the touch of the unfinished—give the illusion that the drawing is finished, but actual finish is reserved for the painting. It is astonishing to see how closely Kaethe Kollwitz, a purely Nordic and Gothic artist, resembles the Italian masters in her creative process, especially after she had changed her style by omissions, shortcuts, and simplifications. A drawing is no doubt a more intimate document than a painting. Gauguin called his drawings "my private letters . . . my secrets," but nevertheless, he was a better painter than a draftsman; Rembrandt and Goya, artists who had a deep influence on the work of Kaethe Kollwitz, achieved the same autonomous level in their painting, drawing, and etching.

Rembrandt's early drawings, following Caravaggio's school, were black or red chalk studies of individual figures of beggars and old men. "These penetrating studies after life are different from the studies of Italian artists by the fact that the interest lies not alone in the control of the formal problem of presentation, but also in the artist's manifested deep human interest in his models; the mere study in Rembrandt's hands is transformed at once into a character study."[1] Kaethe Kollwitz approached Rembrandt's character studies through this same deep interest in her models, and, later in her life, through the elimination of details, turning costume into abstract vestment. Kaethe Kollwitz' drawings are the highest artistic expression of her powerful *Formensprache.*

Shortly after World War II, a large number of Kollwitz drawings found their way to this country, and a number of these are published in this book for the first time. Others have been added in an attempt to trace her creative process from the "first idea" to a more finished form, and to show the extraordinary interrelationship between her work and her life.

A more comprehensive book on the drawings of such a great artist was a necessity. This is the first publication in English which deals exclusively with Kaethe Kollwitz's drawings. It is hoped that the book will serve to broaden the knowledge and understanding of this unique artist and the forces which have shaped her work.

Thanks for permission to reproduce drawings from their collections are due to: The National Gallery of Art, Washington, D.C.; Lessing J. Rosenwald; Elizabeth Mongan, Curator of Drawings and Prints of the National Gallery of Art and the Lessing Rosenwald Collection; Paul J. Sachs, Professor Emeritus of Fine Arts, Harvard University, Agnes Mongan, Curator of Drawings of the Fogg Art Museum, Harvard University; Adelyne D. Breeskin, Director of the Baltimore Museum of Art; Mr. and Mrs. Erich Cohn, New York; Dr. Otto Kallir; Hildegard Bachert of the Galerie St. Etienne, New York; and to all other public collections and private collectors; also to Henry Regnery for giving permission to quote from his publication *Diaries and Letters of Kaethe Kollwitz,* a unique source book, and to Harold Hugo of the Meriden Gravure Company and a director of the American Institute of Graphic Arts, for his painstaking effort to reproduce as many drawings as possible directly from the originals.

Further thanks for advice and help are due to: Mrs. Rudolf Pierre Wendel; Mr. and Mrs. George Grosz; Susanne M. Kresse-Schlensog; Abe Lerner, Art Director of The World Publishing Company; Walter D. Brownfield; Dr. Gerd Muehsam, Librarian of the Cooper Union; Dr. Iris Mueller, Professor of English Literature, Finch College, New York, for her editorial cooperation; William Lieberman, Curator of Prints of the Museum of Modern Art; A. Hyatt Mayor, Curator of Prints of the Metropolitan Museum of Art and President of the Hispanic Society of America. H.B.

New York, April 16, 1959

CONTENTS


| | |
|---|---|
| Foreword | ix |
| Life | 1 |
| Notes | 16 |
| Bibliography | 17 |
| Catalog | 19 |
| Plates | 37 |

# KAETHE KOLLWITZ DRAWINGS

# LIFE

THE SUBSTANCE OF KAETHE KOLLWITZ'S ART IS DOMINATED BY COMPASSION, strength, and self control. This compassion has nothing to do with *Schwermut* or *Wehmut,* or with the weakness of a sentimental heart. Her strength is the deep understanding of the misery of her neighbors, the oppressed and downtrodden—the mothers, the young and old men, the children—and their poverty, hunger, sorrow, and death. She demonstrates her self control in a great number of self portraits, which, in her later years bear traces of dry and silent tears on her kind face, her monumental visage.

A great dramatist—despite her use of only the means and techniques of the graphic artist (drawing, etching, lithography, woodcut) and, later on, of the sculptor —she invents her own stage, in the sense of the Greek tragedy, on which her *dramatis personae* tread the boards. While the art of the Italian painters of the Renaissance supported, in a thousand forms and colors, the high ideals of the Roman Catholic Church, she dared to create through her art, in black and white, the idea of a united brotherhood of mankind, and thus became their forerunner and torchbearer in art.

Kaethe Kollwitz was born on July 8, 1867, in Koenigsberg, East Prussia, the fifth child of her parents. Her father, Karl Schmidt, an ardent and radical Social Democrat, had studied law but soon became aware that in the era of Radowitz and Bismarck, a career for a Social Democrat in the Prussian kingdom would be impossible. He started to learn stone-masonry, soon became a master mason, and, later on a successful house builder.

Kaethe's mother, Katherina Schmidt, was the daughter of Julius Rupp, an ordained Lutheran pastor, who was expelled from the official State Church and founded, in 1846, the first Free Congregation, a renitent community whose services and rites were closer to those of the earliest Christian communities and whose ministers received no remuneration from the State, but were independent.

The youth of Kaethe Kollwitz was serene and sunny. She played with her older brother Konrad, her sisters, and the neighbors' children in the courtyard of a large house near the Pregel River, where her father kept horses and carriages and where bricks for the new buildings were unloaded from barges. Nearby was the shop of a man who made plaster casts whom she often watched at his work. The meadows of the Pregel and, during vacations, the Baltic Sea and the Samland were the surroundings for her youthful recreation.

Grandfather Rupp and her parents were opposed to public schools, so the girls were sent to small private institutions. Kaethe did not enjoy school, but her Grandfather's lessons in religion and socialism were to have a great influence on her education. She was only five or six when she started to draw on scraps of blueprint paper which her father gave to the children. He soon started to collect those scraps of paper.

A lasting impression was made on Kaethe by the early death of her younger brother, Benjamin. Her early childhood was not free from anxieties and nocturnal fears. She often worried that something might happen to her mother, that she might drown while taking her bath in the family tub. Sometimes she began to cry and howl stubbornly, an outburst which was dreaded by the entire family.

Her father was quick to recognize her artistic potentials and wanted to provide her with the best training available. She was twelve years old when she began her lessons in drawing and copying plastercasts. Her first teachers in Koenigsberg were an engraver named Maurer and, later, the well-known *genre* painter, Emil Neide, who came from the school of Wilhelm Dietz. She took great pleasure in those lessons and immediately became a conscientious and hard-working pupil.

Classical German literature was an important part of Kaethe's family life. One of her aunts knew the whole of Klopstock's *Messiah* by heart. Their bookshelves contained the complete works of Goethe with engravings by Bonaventura Genelli, the works of Schiller, Schwab's *Myths and Epics of Classical Antiquity,* especially the poet Freiligrath, and even Kleist. The children staged performances with theatrical paper-dolls and scenery made of building blocks. They were allowed to indulge fully their imaginative love of fantasy. Goethe was always to remain Kaethe's favorite poet.

Twelve-year-old Kaethe exchanged childish kisses in the cellar of her home with her first boy friend, Otto Kunzemueller. They called those kisses "refreshments." In her memoirs, she wrote:

> After this first infatuation of mine, I was always in love. It was a chronic condition; sometimes it was only a gentle undertone to my ordinary life, and sometimes it took stronger hold of me. I was not particularly discriminating about the objects of my love. I fell in love with women. Rarely did the person I was in love with have the slightest suspicion of my feelings. At the same time, I was plunged into those states of an indefinite longing for I knew not of the torments that a child experiences at puberty.[2]

She was about sixteen when she made her first characteristic drawings of working people—types which she saw in her father's offices, longshoremen and sailors on ships and fruit barges of the Koenigsberg Pregel harbor, and peasants. Her great narrative gift, during the first half of her life, was influenced by works of literature. A few drawings were inspired by Ferdinand Freiligrath's poem, *The Emigrants.*

When Kaethe was seventeen, her mother had to go to a Swiss spa for her health. Her father decided that she and her younger sister, Lise, should accompany their mother. During a short stay in Berlin, they met the then still unknown poet, Gerhart Hauptmann, who was a neighbor of Kaethe's older sister in Erkner, a suburb of Berlin. The voyage was also intended to introduce the two girls to Berlin and Munich. In

Munich, Kaethe was tremendously impressed by the paintings of Rubens in the *Alte Pinacothek*. They continued to St. Moritz in the Engadin and from there, in a small cart, to the Malloggia Pass from which Kaethe glimpsed Italy with longing eyes. But her mother insisted that she must return to Koenigsberg to take care of her father. Her desire to see Italy was not fulfilled until twenty-three years later.

At home, Kaethe was to continue her advanced art studies. At that time no academies or colleges were open to girls, even to especially gifted ones. Finally, arrangements were made for her to continue her work in Berlin, at an art school for women. She was extremely fortunate to find a teacher who had a full understanding of her extraordinary talent, Karl Stauffer-Bern, a friend of the sculptor and etcher, Max Klinger. Stauffer-Bern was a great Swiss artist, an enemy of everything indefinite and vague, a first rate draftsman and etcher whose sense of light and shade gave a sculptural roundness to his famous portraits.

While Kaethe was painting, he called her attention again and again to the importance of drawing. She showed him her drawings for Freiligrath's *Emigrants,* a somewhat sentimental poem which expresses the sorrows of German emigrants driven away from the Black Forest for political reasons. Those drawings must have been much stronger and better than the poem for Stauffer-Bern said to her: "But that is Klinger!" Never having heard of Max Klinger, she immediately went to a gallery where his large folio etchings were on exhibition. Those etchings, their technique and especially their interpretation of social oppression and injustice, became a revelation. It was the first time that she found a reflection of her own ideas and feelings in another's work. As her eminent biographer and critic, Willy Kurth, wrote: "Kaethe Kollwitz often called the three etchings known as *Dramas* (Opus IX), her spiritual and artistic birth."[3]

Despite her dedication to her art, she became engaged at seventeen to Karl Kollwitz, a medical student in Berlin who was a childhood friend of her brother, Konrad. Her father doubted that she could fulfill the duties of a doctor's wife and at the same time pursue the hard work of a prominent artist, which he believed she was destined to become.

She still wanted to paint and her father sent her to Munich where she studied under Ludwig Herterich in the Woman's Art School from 1888 to 1889. Herterich, also of the school of William Dietz, emphasized painting and color, but not drawing. Kaethe later said that she learned how "to see" through Herterich.[4] However, she started to feel that color was not her medium. So many students in her class were better colorists. In a school competition, she selected a scene from Zola's *Germinal,* a novel about coal miners, to illustrate the theme of "struggle." This black-and-white composition was unanimously acclaimed and her hope and faith in herself were highly strengthened and confirmed.

At this time, she happened to read Max Klinger's pamphlet, *Painting and Drawing,*[5] in which he writes that certain motives and themes can be completely and artistically interpreted in drawings, but are inartistic in painting. Believing that drawing and the graphic arts (*Griffelkunst*) best express the darker aspects of life, he supplemented Lessing's doctrine defined in *Laokoon or the Limitations of Painting and Poetry*. In his text, Klinger placed the possibilities of the graphic arts on the same autonomous level as those of the art of painting—a doctrine similar to the one Duerer had already proved with his famous engravings and woodcuts.

When, in 1890, Kaethe returned to Koenigsberg, her leaning toward the graphic arts became more definite. After selling one of her early *genre* paintings, *Before the Ball,* she rented her first small studio and continued to sketch peasants, workers, longshoremen, and sailors in the dock taverns on the Pregel quays. Brushes and palette moved more and more in the background as she became convinced that she could express her powerful visions and ideas better in black and white.

In 1891, she was married to Dr. Karl Kollwitz, who, by this time, had established himself in the north of Berlin as a *Kassenarzt,* a doctor who participated in an early form of socialized medical care for the poorer classes. The couple settled in a large apartment at 25 Weissenburgerstrasse, Berlin N. 58. This house remained Kaethe Kollwitz's residence until it was destroyed in World War II.

In 1892, her first son, Hans, was born and in 1896, her second son, Peter. Between these two happy events was another which became the turning point in Kaethe's artistic development and which she herself recalled as making a "tremendous impression." This was the first performance of Gerhart Hauptmann's drama "The Weavers," produced under the direction of Otto Brahm on the Freie Volksbuehne with the great actress, Else Lehmann, in the role of Mother Baumart. This naturalistic drama, which made the poet world famous, describes the misery and injustice endured by the Silesian weavers in Langenbielau and their doomed revolt in 1842.

Kaethe Kollwitz returned home from this performance so deeply moved that she dropped her work on the etchings which she had started for *Germinal* and began her preliminary drawings for the great etching cycle, "The Weavers." This epic creation took her almost five years. According to Klipstein's Oeuvre Catalogue, she rejected six etched plates. In her drive for perfection she found her etching technique still unsatisfactory. The final form of the cycle encompassed six works. Three were lithographs: "Poverty," "Death," and "Conspiracy," Three were etchings with aquatint and sandpaper: "March of the Weavers," "Riot," and "The End." This cycle was not an explicit illustration of stage setting for the drama. It became a free and powerful naturalistic apotheosis of the misery, hope, courage, decision, and doom of the suffering people unfolded in Hauptmann's tragedy.

A final sheet, an allegorical tryptich, "The Downtrodden," which she had planned as plate 7, was omitted at the advice of Julius Elias, since it still showed traces of Klinger's pseudo-romantic influence. It was this art critic, Julius Elias, who had discovered her when she showed some of her work in an independent exhibition,

The Union of the Eleven, after it was refused by the official jury of the Moabiter Glaspalast in Berlin. He wrote at that time: "Almost all visitors seem to have overlooked the decisive talent of a young woman who will be able to bear the insult of the first refusal much easier, since she can be sure of a rich artistic future. . . ."[6]

Kaethe Kollwitz dedicated "The Weavers," her most widely acclaimed production, to her father, who was overjoyed when she presented him with a complete set on the occasion of his seventieth birthday. The cycle was finally shown to the public in the Great Exhibition at the Lehrter Bahnhof in Berlin in the summer of 1898,

KÄTE KOLLWITZ, ARBEITER, VOM BAHNHOF KOMMEND

HOMECOMING WORKERS AT THE LEHRTER BAHNHOF. wash, 1899

after his death. Among the jury committee were Max Liebermann and the great and distinguished Adolf Menzel, then the leading personality of the Berlin art world. Despite his eighty-three years, he was full of vigor and independent judgment. He proposed the small gold medal be awarded to the artist of "The Weavers." But the presentation of this honor was suppressed by Emperor Wilhelm II who, notwithstanding his adoration of Menzel, disliked what he called "gutter art" (*Rinnstein Kunst*). The acquisition of a set by the Berlin Kupferstichkabinet, however, could not be avoided, even if the acquisition was not officially mentioned on the labels in deference to the Kaiser.

In 1889, Max Lehrs, then director of the Print Room in Dresden, exhibited the cycle, and the King of Saxony, a more liberal monarch who occasionally liked to antagonize the Emperor, awarded the medal to Kaethe Kollwitz.

In 1901, she created an exceptionally large etching, "The Carmagnole" (Dance Around the Guillotine), an astonishing example of the artist's feeling for music, dance, and rhythm. It was inspired by a passage from Charles Dickens' *A Tale of Two Cities:* "There was *no other* music than their own singing. They danced to the popular revolution song, keeping a ferocious time that was like a gnashing of teeth in unison." Kaethe Kollwitz emphasized the rhythmic strength of this revolutionary dance by adding a drummer boy. Her wish to emphasize this drummer boy, who in her first draft seems to be only a bearded old man, obliged her to make a half lifesize drawing of this boy, who with his drum drives the dance of those desperate and erratic women to a culminating point of hatred and annihilation.

Some biographers believe that Kaethe Kollwitz's second great cycle, "Peasant War," was inspired by Hauptmann's second drama of the masses, *Florian Geyer.* However, the performance of this drama in 1896, did not leave a great impression on her. The Peasant War was a violent revolution against the nobility and the church in many parts of Southern Germany in the early years of the Reformation beginning in 1525. Its cause was the inhuman treatment of the peasants who were virtually slaves without property—or owners of a few acres of land—forced by their feudal lords to compulsory services and burdened with excessive taxes. It was not Hauptmann's drama, but rather an imaginative play of her youth, in which she and her brother Konrad were barricade fighters in an imaginary revolution, that provided the original source of her interest. Furthermore, Zimmermann's *General History of the Great Peasant War* mentions a woman called Black Anne who incited the peasants to their uprising. She identified herself with this woman, and the idea occupied her for a long time. Characteristically, she started the cycle with the fifth sheet, "Outbreak," with the marvelous figure of Black Anne as protagonist (see plate 22). On the basis of this sheet the cycle was ordered by the Society for Historical Art. Struggling with an exuberance of ideas and themes, making preliminary and more finished drawings, attempting and rejecting several scenes in lithography, she worked on this cycle from 1902 to 1908. When it was finally published, "Peasant War" (see plates 22-36) consisted of seven sheets in etching, acquatint, and soft ground: "Plowing," "Raped," "Sharpening the Scythe," "Arming in the Vault," "Outbreak," "After the Battle," and "The Prisoners." With the exception of plate 2, "Raped," which still shows a slight trace of Klinger's overflowing style *(Jugendstil),* the cycle, larger in size than "The Weavers," towers over her first popular work through the impact of its strength, dramatization, lights, halftones, and shadows. It was a culmination point in her technique as an etcher.

During her work on "Peasant War," she visited Paris twice. The city with its atmosphere, museums, its magic, and artistic flavor, enchanted her. For a short time she frequented the morning classes at the Académie Julian where she made her first attempts at sculpture. She visited Rodin twice, in his studios in Paris and Meudon, and was a guest in Steinlen's studio. On her return trip, she planned to see the sculptor Constantin Meunier with whom she felt a kinship. It was Meunier who said to Max Lehrs, when he saw the drawing for the right wing of "The Downtrodden": "I have never seen such a drawing by the hand of a woman." Unfortunately, she could not go to Brussels and Meunier died soon after.

The etching "Outbreak" received the Villa Romana prize, which was awarded to her by Max Klinger. The prize provided for a full year's sojourn in Florence. In 1907, accompanied by her younger son Peter, she left for Italy. In her "Retrospect," 1941, she wrote:

> Supposedly the artists would also carry on their own work. I did not work at all although I was given a handsome studio in the Villa Romana. But there, for the first time, I began to understand Florentine art.[7]

After her husband had visited her for a short time, taking Peter home with him, she took a walking tour along the Ligurian coast from Florence to Rome accompanied by a highly sympathetic lady friend, Stan-Harding-Krayl. She did not see Perugia and Assisi, as she had originally planned. Since she had studied early Renaissance paintings in Florence so carefully, she was deeply impressed by the frescoes of Masaccio in Santa Maria del Carmine—it is to be regretted that, like her favorite poet Goethe 121 years before, she failed to see the frescoes by Cimabue, Giotto, Lorenzetti, and Simone Martini in the lower and upper Church of St. Francis in Assisi.

The two friends arrived in Rome in June, 1907. "The superabundance of classical and medieval art was almost frightening."[8] Time was running short and they saw but little. The family had planned to meet in La Spezia and go to the little fishing village of Fiascherino. There they enjoyed a glorious vacation and celebrated mother's fortieth birthday. Finally, they returned home.

Later, Kaethe Kollwitz wrote: "My life between thirty and forty was very happy in every respect."[9] It has often been said that her journey to Italy made no impression on her work and style. It is true that she was a Gothic and Nordic artist and the character of her art had already reached a ripened and definite form. But under the influence of a long stay in this country full of the most sublime works of art, and the further influences of rising new tendencies of the younger generation in Germany —the Expressionists, the Bauhaus, and the Blue Four—the feeling tormented her often, in long periods of depression and inability to work, that in order to progress she had to find a new style, a new form.

By 1909, she had finished the set of drawings for the periodical *Simplicissimus* which the editor entitled "Pictures of Misery" *(Bilder vom Elends).* Due to her fundamental experience, she was now able to express whatever she wanted to without models. However, at the end of 1909, she wrote in her diaries:

> On Saturday the Secession was opened. I went there with Hans. My things were hung

well, although the etchings were separate. Nevertheless I am no longer satisfied. There are too many good things there that seem fresher than mine. Brandenburg is excellent this time. I wish I had done his dance, his orgy. In my own work I find that I must try to keep everything to a more and more abbreviated form. The execution seems to be too complete. I should like to do the new etchings so that all the essentials are strongly stressed and the inessentials almost omitted.[10]

In this move toward simplified form, a step forward was made in her etchings—"Runover" (K. 104), 1910; her "Self-Portrait," already with snow-white hair (K. 122), 1912; the lithographs—"March Cemetery" (K. 125), 1913, and "Waiting" (K.126), 1914. A culmination of this new abbreviated style can be found in such a masterpiece as "Maria and Elizabeth," 1927. With its tenderness, delicacy, strength, and further omission of detail, it shows that she had not forgotten the frescoes of the Italian early Renaissance.

In 1910, she began to work more on sculpture. But she was not only the disciplined, dedicated artist. She was also the wife of a doctor who practiced medicine in one of the poorest districts of the north of Berlin. With her great heart she identified herself with the fate and burdens of the oppressed and heavyladen, especially the mothers. She suffered with them in their grief—in birth, life, and death. Her sympathy was so strong that she gave her own form and features to most of the women she drew and took under the protective wings of her art.

Her husband shared her dedication to social work and her marriage to Karl Kollwitz was also, in this sense, a fulfillment. In the introduction to her diaries, her son, Hans Kollwitz, wrote:

Mother would see anyone who wanted to call on her, although these visits often sapped her strength. People would bring their griefs and problems to her and usually left feeling relieved. But then *she* would have one more burden to bear. That was the way she usually helped people.[11]

In a heartbreaking entry in her diary of one of those visits she reveals the tragic milieu which had become the subject of her art:

Frau Pankopf was here. She had a black eye. Her husband had flown into a rage. When I asked her about him, she said he had wanted to be a teacher, but had become a worker in tortoise-shell and was well paid for his work. His heart became enlarged, and at the same time he had his first attacks of extreme restlessness. He went for treatment and then tried to work again. It wouldn't do; he tried to get other work; and last winter went about with a hurdy-gurdy. His feet swelled, and the longer it went on the more he suffered from melancholy and nervousness. Wailed continuously that he longed for death, could not support his family, and so on. When their next to the last child died, he remained in a hysterical misery much longer than his wife. Six of the children are living. Finally he started to have fits of rage and was taken to Herzbierge [an asylum near Berlin]. The more I see of it, the more I realize that this is the *typical* misfortune of the workers' families. As soon as the man drinks or is sick and unemployed it is always the same story. . . . For the woman the misery is always the same. She keeps the children whom she must feed, scolds and complains about her husband. She sees only what has become of him and not how he became that way.[12]

No hint can be found in her diaries and letters of the menacing clouds of the outbreak of World War I.

"Great piercing arrows have not yet struck me; my darling boys are growing more independent."[13] As soon as the war started in August, 1914, her younger son, Peter, volunteered. He was eighteen years of age and impassioned by his ideas and his sense of duty. He was killed on October 22, 1914, at Dixmuiden in Flanders as the first of his regiment. The pain his mother suffered was an ordeal which overshadowed her through her remaining years. In December of 1914, she made the first drawings for a monumental memorial for Peter and his dead comrades, a work which she broke up in 1919, only to start on it again in 1925 after a long delay.

In 1916, she exhibited her first sculpture, which she had begun before the death of her son, in the Free Secession. On the occasion of her fiftieth birthday, the Free Secession opened, in the galleries of Paul Cassirer, a large retrospective exhibition of one hundred and fifty Kollwitz drawings. Selecting the material for the exhibit out of the wealth of her studio collection, she complained about her early drawings as being too narrative or anecdotal. We know little about the early period. This retrospective exhibition mainly showed drawings made after her Munich years, and most of her earlier work may have been destroyed later when her house was bombed during World War II. Willy Kurth wrote a beautiful review of this exhibition where a few sculptures were also shown:

> Only the exhibition of one hundred and fifty drawings, arranged in honor of the fiftieth birthday of the artist, gives them an independent character, the value of a "work." The elements of her nature and her art can often be felt more immediately in the drawings than in the prints, even much that in the latter has scarcely found a fulfillment.[14]

Shortly before the end of World War I, the poet Richard Dehmel wrote, in October, 1918, a last stirring appeal to the German nation calling old men and young boys for a last resistance as the only salvation of the fatherland. Friedrich Stampfer, the courageous editor-in-chief of the newspaper *Vorwaerts* printed it, but asked Kaethe Kollwitz for an answer first. She wrote an inflammatory reply which ended:

> There has been enough of dying! Let not another man fall! Against Richard Dehmel, I ask that the works of an even greater poet [Goethe] be remembered: "Seed for the planting must not be ground."[15]

Her letter was printed in the *Vorwaerts* as well as in the *Vossische Zeitung*.

While working on the etching and the lithograph of "The Mothers" (K. 134 and K. 135), and on her significant memorial sheet for Karl Liebknecht, in soft ground (K. 137), and in lithography (K. 138), she went to the exhibitions of the Secession. There she saw for the first time the woodcuts of Ernst Barlach. They overwhelmed her. Since she was disappointed with transfer lithography, had trouble in

MONUMENT IN ROGGEVELDE: *The Father*. Photo, Mrs. Erich Cohn.

getting lithographic stones into the studio, and found etching inadequate to express her monumental concepts, she decided, in 1919, to cut her print for Karl Liebknecht in wood (K. 139). It was her first woodcut. By 1926, she had made about thirty. Barlach led her to the new medium, but she felt he did not influence her style, although each admired the other's art.

In 1920, the Weimar Republic elected her a member of the Prussian Academy of Arts. This membership entitled her to a slight regular income, a large studio in the Academy, and a full-fledged professorship. The honor was outstanding for she was the first woman to be elected to the Academy.

In the same year, Max Klinger died. Representing the Free Secession, she attended Klinger's funeral in Gross-Jena where she delivered a remarkable eulogy at his grave and expressed her gratitude toward him.

Returning via the city of Naumburg with her husband, she visited the Cathedral, recording its deep impression later:

> We admired the old sculpture in the Choir and the magnificent stained windows in the other wing of the church. Karl and I came independently to the conclusion: Time would not revive the unity of the Catholic faith, a unity which once encompassed all

MONUMENT IN ROGGEVELDE: *The Mother.* Photo, Mrs. Erich Cohn.

the peoples of Europe. This single strong belief created the churches and made all arts understandable. The arts were one as they had been at the holy places of earlier cultures. The decline of religion brought disintegration until, at last, in our century, the figurative arts have degenerated to the wretchedness of exhibition galleries.[16]

In 1922-23 she completed the cycle "War" for which she had made a number of drawings, and for which she had tried etching and lithography, but which, in the final form, became woodcuts. The titles of this cycle were: "The Sacrifice," "The Volunteers," "The Parents," "The Widow I," The Widow II," "The Mothers," and "The People" (K. 177-83). It embodied a work of many years, expressing her reaction to the war of 1914-18. The seven woodcuts were published in 1924.

During this year she also created her three most famous posters: "Germany's Children Starving" (K. 190), "Bread" (K. 196), and "Never Again War" (K. 200). In addition, she had started to work on her last great cycle, "Death." Like Daumier, Degas, Renoir, and Picasso she had a strong inclination toward and a great talent for sculpture. After a happy sea voyage to Madeira, Funchal, and Teneriffa, she returned to her plans for the monument to Peter to be placed in the soldiers' cemetery of Roggevelde near Dixmuiden in Flanders. She visualized two life-sized mourning and praying figures: "The Father" and "The Mother." To discover the best location for her figures she visited the cemetery and decided to place them just within the entrance with their backs against a tall thick hedge so that they could overlook the whole field lined with small grave crosses.

But again, she was afflicted by deep depression, sudden inhibitions preventing her work; she felt almost too old to accomplish her great task. Often she covered the figures unwrapping them only at long intervals. Sometimes she thought that it might be best to drop the project, but she was too tenacious a fighter and kept on.

Invited by the Soviet Government to visit Russia for the celebration of the tenth anniversary of the Soviet Republic—she had once made a poster for the Russian War Relief (K. 154)—she and her husband made a refreshing trip to that country. This was shortly after her sixtieth birthday. She was then working on a number of woodcuts and lithographs—"Boy Embracing His Mother" (K. 246) which became her most admired and popular print of this period—and on her last two etchings.

In 1931, she finished her two monumental sculptures. The plaster casts were shown in the Academy and the reaction and recognition of her fellow sculptors made her very happy. With her supervision and assistance, the sculptors Diederichs and Rhades carved the statues in Belgian granite. Ludwig Justi, director of the National Gallery, offered to exhibit the granite statues in the atrium of his museum, where they were seen for three weeks by many thousands of people.

The stones were transported to Roggevelde and, under the eyes of Kaethe Kollwitz, were erected at the predetermined place. In her diary she wrote about her farewell to her greatest sculptural work:

> We went from the figures to Peter's grave and everything was alive and wholly felt. I stood before the woman, looked at her—my own face—and wept and stroked her cheeks.[17]

In January, 1933, the Weimar Republic went to pieces and the Hitler regime came to power. Though Kaethe Kollwitz was never a member of any of Germany's political parties, it was to be expected that her work would be outlawed as a symbol of humanity and pacifism as were Romain Rolland's and Albert Schweitzer's. This was done slowly but systematically. First, on February 15, she was obliged to resign from the Academy, but retained the studio and her full salary until October 1, when she was finally expelled. Gradually her art disappeared from the museums and was relegated to basement junk piles together with works of Barlach, George Grosz, Corinth, Liebermann, Schmidt-Rottluff, Nolde, Kokoschka, and Pechstein—to mention only a few. In September, the Gestapo raided her son's home, where, in addition to her own works, Arthur Bonus' monograph *Das Kaethe Kollwitz Werk* was thought to be hidden. Art galleries were officially forbidden to exhibit her work or to handle it, but her plates were sold secretly or smuggled to foreign countries. Despite this an-

THE TWO FIGURES IN ROGGEVELDE. Photo, Mrs. Erich Cohn.

guish, she continued to work silently in her new, much smaller studio. Between 1934 and 1936, she managed to finish her last great lithograph cycle, "Death" (K. 256-63). This series, which had occupied her for a long time, contained eight stones: "Woman Welcoming Death," "Death with Girl in Lap," "Death Reaches for a Group of Children," "Death Struggles with a Woman," "Death on the Highway," "Death as a Friend," "Death in the Water," and "The Call of Death."

In July, 1936, she was interrogated by two officers of the Gestapo about an irrelevant article in *Isvestia* and menaced with arrest and placement in a concentration camp. Intimidated, she and her husband spent the next few days in anguish and anxiety. They had been told about the horrors of those prisons by many people who had relatives there. When they had poured out their hearts she had known that she could not help them, but in her great compassion, she had listened to them.

Having listened only too closely, she and her husband resolved to commit suicide if the concentration camp were to become unavoidable. However, no other threats were made. The Ministry for Propaganda and Enlightenment was well aware that Kaethe Kollwitz was not only a great figure in the German and international art

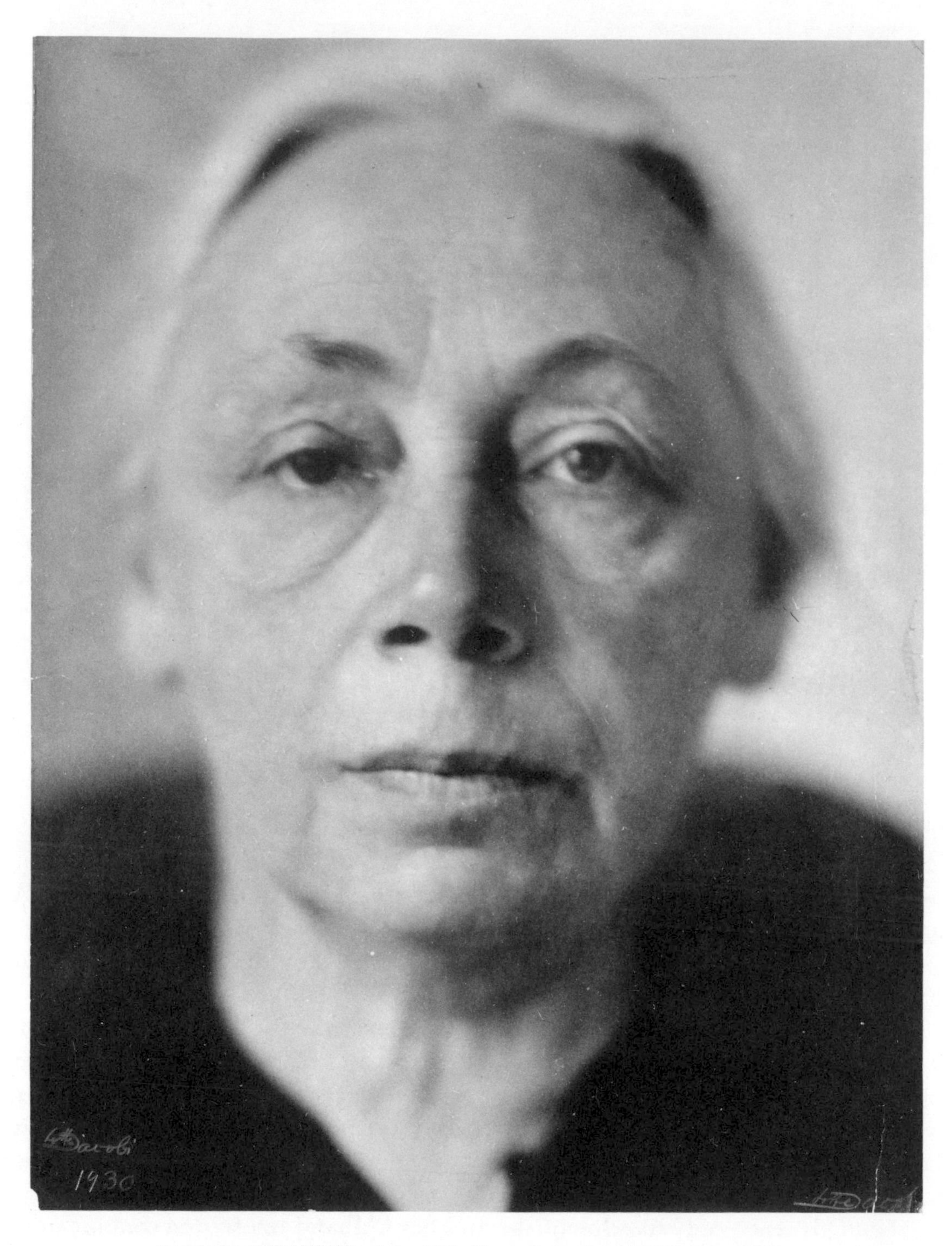


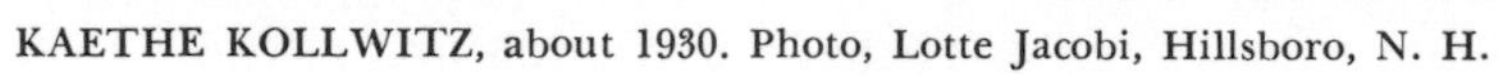

KAETHE KOLLWITZ, about 1930. Photo, Lotte Jacobi, Hillsboro, N. H.

world, but that her name had become a symbol and that her early work was deeply rooted in the hearts of the German people. Since the publication of the inexpensive *Kunstwart* folders, prints from "The Weavers" and the "Carmagnole" could be found in thousands of homes of the German working class.

On her seventieth birthday, the outlawed artist received over one hundred and fifty telegrams from leading personalities of the art world and piles of letters from friends and courageous people who still had to live in the country. Later on, friends, among them Erich Cohn of New York, an ardent collector of her work, offered to bring her out of Germany and to assume all the obligations for her stay in the United States. But she gratefully declined lest an anti-Nazi demonstration bring reprisals to her family.

After the outbreak of World War II, shock followed shock. In 1940, her husband died and she became increasingly frail. In her last "Self-Portrait, with the Profile to the Right" (K. 265), 1941, with her back already bent, she seems to pass by like "a queen in exile." The next year, when her oldest grandson, Peter Kollwitz, was killed in action in Russia, she still had the strength to create her last warning lithograph of the mother protecting her three children: "Seed For The Planting Must Not Be Ground" (K. 267), 1942.

Gradually, the bombing of Berlin became so unbearable that she accepted the invitation of a friend, the sculptress Margarete Boening, to live in Nordhausen, in the Harz Mountains. In November, 1943, her house in Berlin was hit in an air attack which destroyed much irreplaceable material, proof prints, rare states, drawings, letters, and documents. A week later the house of her son, Hans, was also bombed. Then, with the invention of the V-bomb in 1944, Nordhausen had to be evacuated. Prince Ernst Heinrich of Saxony, a collector of drawings, trustee of the large drawing collection of the Wettin family, and a great admirer of her work, invited the artist to the village of Moritzburg near Dresden, where she lived in two rooms at the Ruedenhof estate and where the prince tried to make her now homeless life as bearable as possible. Her granddaughter Jutta stayed with her and her son Hans visited his mother as often as the difficult wartime traveling conditions allowed. It was he who recorded her death:

> My last visit was on Good Friday, 1945. I read Mother the Easter story from the gospel of St. Matthew—which she knew as well as the text of a favorite oratorio. Then I read her the Easter walk from *Faust,* which she so loved. Shattered by age though she was, she seemed like a queen in exile; she had a compelling kindness and dignity. That is the last memory I have of her. My daughter was at her bedside when she died on April 22, 1945. Her last words were, "My greetings to all."[18]

The fame which she wore like a shining mantle could take nothing away from her simplicity. She was the greatest woman artist the world has known so far, a great mother with a still greater heart for all the oppressed and humilated, a woman "of sorrow and acquainted with grief."[19]

# NOTES

1. Charles de Tolnay, *History and Technique of Old Master Drawings,* p. 65.
2. *The Diaries and Letters of Kaethe Kollowitz,* edited by Hans Kollwitz, Chicago, Henry Regnery Company, 1955 (henceforth referred to as *Diaries and Letters*), p. 22.
3. Willy Kurth, "Kaethe Kollwitz," Geleitwort zum *Katalog der Ausstellung in der Deutschen Akademie der Kuenste,* 1951.
4. *Diaries and Letters,* p. 40.
5. Max Klinger, *Malerei und Zeichnung,* 1891.
6. Julius Elias, "Kaethe Kollwitz," *Kunst und Kuenstler,* Vol. 16, Berlin, 1917.
7. *Diaries and Letters,* p. 45.
8. Ibid., p. 46.
9. Ibid., p. 44.
10. Ibid., p. 52.
11. Hans Kollwitz, in his introduction to *Diaries and Letters,* p. 4.
12. *Diaries and Letters,* pp. 51-52.
13. *Diaries and Letters,* p. 54.
14. Willy Kurth, *Kunstchronik,* N.F., Vol. XXXVII, 1917.
15. *Diaries and Letters,* p. 89.
16. Freely translated from Kaethe Kollwitz's "Ich will wirken in dieser Zeit," *Auswahl aus den Tagebüchern und Briefen, aus Graphik, Zeichnungen und Plastik,* Einführung von Friedrich Ahlers-Hestermann, Berlin, Gebr. Mann, 1952, p. 89.
17. *Diaries and Letters,* p. 122.
18. Hans Kollwitz, in his introduction to *Diaries and Letters,* p. 11.
19. Isaiah LIII: 3; G. F. Handel, *Messiah,* Part the Second.

# BIBLIOGRAPHY


## *Oeuvre Catalogues*

KLIPSTEIN, AUGUST. *The Graphic Work of Kaethe Kollwitz;* New York, Galerie St. Etienne, 1955. xx + 360 pp; 277 reproductions; text in German. Complete illustrated catalogue. The section of this book covering the years 1890-1912 is based on the descriptive catalogue by Professor Johannes Sievers, published in 1913.

LEHRS, MAX. "Kaethe Kollwitz," *Die graphischen Kuenste,* Vol. XXVI, pp. 55-67; Vienna, 1910. 7 reproductions; 1 original etching. First list of 50 graphic works from the years 1890-1902.

## *Writings by the Artist*

*The Diaries and Letters of Kaethe Kollwitz;* translated by Richard and Clara Winston; Chicago, Henry Regnery Company, 1955. xii + 212 pp; 48 plates.

*"Ich will wirken in dieser Zeit," Auswahl aus den Tagebüchern und Briefen, aus Graphik, Zeichnungen und Plastik.* Einführung von Friedrich Ahlers-Hestermann. Berlin, Gebr. Mann, 1952. 142 pp.; 52 reproductions.

## *Monographs, Portfolios, Essays, and Reviews*

BIEDRZYNSKI, RICHARD. *Das brennende Gewissen. Maler im Aufstand gegen ihre Zeit. Hogarth, Goya, Daumier, Kollwitz,* pp. 133-69; Braunschweig, Georg Westermann, 1949. 12 reproductions.

BONUS, ARTHUR. *Das Kaethe Kollwitz Werk. Mit einem Brief von Kaethe Kollwitz,* Neue Auflage; Dresden, Carl Reissner, 1925. 38 pp.; 153 reproductions.

ELIAS, JULIUS. "Kaethe Kollwitz," *Kunst und Kuenstler,* Vol. XVI, pp. 540-49; Berlin, 1917. 8 reproductions.

HAUPTMANN, GERHART. *Abschied und Tod. Acht Zeichnungen von Kaethe Kollwitz.* Geleitwort von G. H., Berlin, Propylaen Verlag, 1924. 8 plates.

HEILBORN, ADOLF. *Kaethe Kollwitz. Die Zeichner des Volkes;* Berlin, Rembrandt-Verlag, 1924. 68 pp.; 56 reproductions.

———*Kaethe Kollwitz,* Erw. 4. Auflage, Berlin, Konrad Lemmer, 1949. 92 pp.; 75 reproductions.

ISAACS, EDITH J. R. "Kaethe Kollwitz: Her Life and Art," *Theatre Arts,* New York, November, 1946. Book Review.

KLEIN, RUDOLF. *Max Klinger;* Berlin, Gose and Tetzlaff, 1903. 32 pp.

KLINGER, MAX. *Malerei und Zeichnung;* 1891. Inselbücherei No. 263.

*Kollwitz Kaethe. 24 Handzeichungen in original-getreuen Wiedergaben.* Mit einem Vorwort von N. G. Hartmann, Dresden, Emil Richter, 1920. 4 pp.; 24 collotypes; 1 original lithograph; known as Richter Portfolio.

*Kaethe Kollwitz-Mappe;* hg. vom Kunstwart; Munich, Callwey, C. D. W., 1913. 4 pp.; 2 reproductions; 13 plates.

KURTH, WILLY. "Kaethe Kollwitz's Zeichnungen," *Kunstchronik N.F.,* Vol. XVIII, pp. 309-11, 1917.

———*Kaethe Kollwitz. Geleitwort zum Katalog der Kaethe Kollwitz-Austellung in der Deutschen Akademie der Kunste,* pp. 7-28; Berlin, 1951.

LESSING, GOTTHOLD EPHRAIM. *Laokoon oder ueber die Grenzen der Malerei und Poesie (1766),* Leipzig, Tempel-Verlag, n.d. Lessing's Werke, Vol. VI, pp. 1-150.

McCausland, Elizabeth. *Kaethe Kollwitz. Ten Lithographs;* New York, Henry C. Kleemann, Curt Valentin, 1941. 4 pp.; 10 plates.

Muller, J. "Kaethe Kollwitz," *Allgemeines Lexikon der Bildenden Kuenstler,* hg. von Ulrich Thieme und Felix Becker, Vol. XXI, pp. 245-47; Leipzig, E. A. Seemann, 1927.

Pan. *Verlegt und herausgeg, von der Genossenschaft Pan,* Vol. V, Part 2, p. 177; 1899.

Schmalenbach, Fritz. *Kaethe Kollwitz,* hg. und eingeleitet von F. Sch. Bern, Renaissance Verlag (H. Engler), 1948. 28 pp.; 83 plates.

Schumann, Werner. *Kaethe Kollwitz. Ein Herz Schlaegt fuer die Mütter;* Hannover, Fackelträger-Verlag, 1953. 94 pp.; 100 reproductions.

Singer, H. W. "Ueber die Zeichnungen von Kaethe Kollwitz," *Mitteilungen aus den Saechsischen Kunstsammlungen,* Vol. III, pp. 96-98; 1912.

Stampfer, Friedrich. *Ein Kollwitz-Buch. Tragödie der Menschheit und einer grossen Frau;* New York, Neue Volkszeitung, August 31, 1946. Book Review.

Tolnay, Charles de. *History and Technique of Old Master Drawings: A Handbook;* New York, H. Bittner and Company, 1943. 170 pp.; 216 reproductions on 120 plates.

Zigrosser, Carl. *Kaethe Kollwitz;* New York, H. Bittner and Company, 1946. 28 pp.; 72 reproductions on 62 plates (Bittner Art Monographs, Vol. VII).

# CATALOG

K. followed by a number refers to the catalog raisonné by August Klipstein, *The Graphic Work of Kaethe Kollwitz,* New York, 1955, describing the etchings, lithographs, and woodcuts for which a number of drawings were preliminary studies.

Dimensions are given in centimeters and inches, but had to be omitted where the originals could not be obtained.

A *Frontispiece*
SELF PORTRAIT
SELBSTBILDNIS
Bronze. Height 36 cm.; 14 3/16 in. 1936. Collection: Erich Cohn, New York.

1 STUDY OF A MAN
SKIZZE EINES MANNES

Pen. 21.6 x 30.2 cm.; 18½ x 11⅝ in. Signed and dated: Kollwitz Studie 1891. National Gallery of Art, Washington, D.C., Rosenwald Collection.

2 SELF PORTRAIT AT THE TABLE WITH HER FUTURE HUSBAND, DR. KARL KOLLWITZ
SELBSTBILDNIS MIT IHREM SPAETEREN GATTEN, DR. KARL KOLLWITZ

Pen and wash. 29.5 x 27.5 cm.; 11⅝ x 10⅞ in. Signed and dated: Schmidt (Kollwitz) Muenchen 1889. Collection: Dr. and Mrs. Otto Kallir, New York.

The signature is of much later date and was probably added in 1917 for the exhibition of 150 drawings in Berlin honoring the fiftieth birthday of Kaethe Kollwitz.

3 KAETHE KOLLWITZ WITH SON, HANS
KAETHE KOLLWITZ MIT SOHN HANS

Wash, pen, and ink. 20.5 x 27.3 cm.; 8 x 10¾ in. Signed: Kollwitz 94, 1894. Collection: Unknown. Richter Portfolio plate 2.

4 INTERIOR FOR "THE WEAVERS"
INTERIEUR FUER "DIE WEBER"

Sepia and pen. 43.4 x 37.7 cm.; 17⅛ x 14⅞ in. Signed: Kaethe Kollwitz, 1894. Collection: Erich Cohn, New York.

5 SIX MEN AT THE TABLE
BERATUNG

Sepia and black wash. 33 x 44.4 cm.; 13 x 17½ in. Signed: Kaethe Kollwitz. About 1893. Collection: Dr. and Mrs. Otto Kallir, New York.

Probably study for plate 3 of "The Weavers" (K. 36). The Signature is of a much later date.

6 DEATH
TOD

Drawing for plate 2 of "The Weavers." Wash heightened with white on yellowish paper. 25.7 x 22.1 cm.; 10⅛ x 8¾ in. Signed and dated: Kollwitz 1897. Collection: Unknown. Richter Portfolio plate 5.

Wash drawing for the lithograph K. 35. Reversed.

7 STORM
STURM

Drawing for plate 5 of "The Weavers" (K. 33). Underneath: Sketch of Two Heads and a Figure. Pencil and charcoal. 58.4 x 43.8 cm.; 23 x 17¼ in. Signed: Kaethe Kollwitz. 1897. Collection: Dr. and Mrs. Otto Kallir, New York.

Reversed.

8 MARCHING WEAVERS
WEBERZUG

Drawing for plate 4 of "The Weavers" (K. 32). Charcoal, pen, and pencil on white paper. 28.6 x 31.1 cm.; 11¼ x 12⅜ in. Signed: Kaethe Kollwitz. 1897. Collection: Dr. and Mrs. Otto Kallir, New York.

Reversed. The signature is of a much later date.

9 THE END
ENDE

Drawing for plate 6 of "The Weavers" (K. 37). Charcoal. 26 x 29.8 cm.; 10¼ x 11¾ in. Signed and dated: Kollwitz 1896. Collection: Dr. and Mrs. Otto Kallir, New York.

Reversed.

10 STUDY OF A WOMAN FOR "DOWNTRODDEN"
FRAUENSTUDIE ZU "ZERTRETENE"

Pen and charcoal. 41.9 x 25.3 cm.; 16½ x 10 in. Unsigned. 1900. Formerly Kupferstichkabinett, Dresden. Richter Portfolio plate 4.

Study for K. 48. Reversed.

11 STUDY OF A CHILD FOR "DOWNTRODDEN"
KINDERSTUDIE FUER "ZERTRETENE"

Pencil. 20.9 x 20.9 cm.; 8¼ x 8¼ in. Signed and dated: Kollwitz I 1900. Formerly Kupferstichkabinett, Dresden. Richter Portfolio plate 3.

Study for a detail of the left side of the triptych K. 48.

12 GRETCHEN
GRETCHEN

Pen and wash. 20.3 x 12.7 cm.; 8 x 5 in. Signed: Kollwitz 99 Gretchen. 1899. Collection: Erich Cohn, New York.

Study for the etching K. 43. Reversed.

13 WOMAN PEELING POTATOES
FRAU KARTOFFELN SCHAELEND

Pen and ink on white paper. 42.5 x 27.9 cm.; 16¾ x 11 in. Signed: Kollwitz. About 1900. Collection: Mr. and Mrs. Matthew H. Futter, New York.

14 SCOLDING MOTHER
SCHELTENDE FRAU

Pen. Signed: Kaethe Kollwitz. About 1900. Collection: Meta and Paul J. Sachs, Fogg Museum of Art, Harvard University, Cambridge, Mass.

Signature added at a later date.

15 MOTHER WITH TWO CHILDREN
MUTTER MIT ZWEI KINDERN

Pen and ink on white paper. 34.9 x 29.2 cm.; 13¾ x 11½ in. Signed: Kollwitz. About 1900. Collection: Robert J. Mayer, New York.

16 THE CARMAGNOLE (DANCE AROUND THE GUILLOTINE)
DIE CARMAGNOLE (TANZ UM DIE GUILLOTINE)

Charcoal. 60 x 45 cm.; 23⅝ x 17¾ in. About 1901. Private Collection, Hamburg.

Probably the first draft for the famous plate K. 49. Reversed.

17 THE CARMAGNOLE (DANCE AROUND THE GUILLOTINE)
DIE CARMAGNOLE (TANZ UM DIE GUILLOTINE)

Charcoal. 46.3 x 37.5 cm.; 18¼ x 14¾ in. Signed: Kaethe Kollwitz. 1901. Collection: Mr. Joseph Katz, Baltimore, Maryland.

Early draft for K. 49. Reversed.

18 STUDY FOR THE CARMAGNOLE
STUDIE ZUR CARMAGNOLE

Pencil. 1901. Formerly Private Collection, Dresden. Richter Portfolio plate 9.

Later draft for K. 49. Reversed.

19 DRUMMER BOY
TROMMELJUNGE

Large detail for "The Carmagnole." Pencil and charcoal heightened with white and pen, on three pieces of yellowish paper. 58.4 x 25.4 cm.; 23 x 10 in. Signed: Kollwitz. 1901. Collection: George Efron, New York.

Study for K. 49. Reversed.

20 PIETA
PIETA

Charcoal and crayon. 47.6 x 69.8 cm.; 18¾ x 27½ in. Signed: Kaethe Kollwitz. 1903. Collection: Lester Jay New, Beverly Hills, California.

Drawing for the lithograph in two colors K. 70.

21 MOTHER WITH DEAD CHILD
FRAU MIT TOTEM KIND

Charcoal and tempera on green paper. 32.4 x 34.3 cm.; 12¾ x 13½ in. Signed: Kaethe Kollwitz. 1903. Collection: Mr. and Mrs. Walter Bareiss, Greenwich, Connecticut.

Study for K. 72.

22 OUTBREAK
LOSBRUCH

Study for plate 5 of the "Peasant War." Charcoal on yellowish paper. 47.3 x 37 cm.; 18⅝ x 14 ⅝ in. Signed: Kaethe Kollwitz. 1903. Formerly Private Collection, Dresden. Richter Portfolio plate 6.

Study for the etching K. 66.

23 STANDING WOMAN
STEHENDE FRAU

Pencil. 43.2 x 21.6 cm.; 17 x 8½ in. Signed: Kollwitz. 1905. National Gallery of Art, Washington, D. C., Rosenwald Collection.

Study for "Ploughman with Standing Woman in the Foreground" (K. 92). Rejected plate from "Peasant War." Reversed.

24 WOMAN WITH SCYTHE
FRAU MIT SENSE

Charcoal and white crayon. 44.4 x 25.4 cm.; 17½ x 10 in. Unsigned. 1905. Collection: Erich Cohn, New York.

Sketch for an aquatint etching for "Peasant War" (K. 89). Reversed. Later on rejected in the cycle.

25 WOMAN WITH SCYTHE
FRAU MIT SENSE

Wash and crayon on gray paper. 40.6 x 22.8 cm.; 16 x 9 in. Signed: Kaethe Kollwitz. 1905. Collection: Erich Cohn, New York.

Sketch for an aquatint etching for "Peasant War" (K. 89). Reversed. Later on rejected in the cycle.

26 WOMAN ON THE BENCH
FRAU AUF DER BANK

Crayon and Chinese ink on brownish paper. 49.5 x 62.2 cm.; 19½ x 24½ in. Signed and dated: Kaethe Kollwitz 1905. Collection: Erich Cohn, New York.

27 HOME WORKER
HEIMARBEITERIN

Charcoal on yellowish paper. 58.2 x 44 cm.; 22⅞ x 17⅝ in. Signed: Kollwitz. 1905. Collection: Unknown. Richter Portfolio plate 17.

Drawing for the poster of the "German Homeworkers' Exhibition," Berlin, 1906 (K. 93). Reversed.

28 MEN STORMING UP STEPS
BEWAFFNUNG IN EINEM GEWOELBE

Drawing for plate 4 of "Peasant War." Charcoal heightened with white. 46.4 x 31.2 cm.; 18¼ x 12¼ in. Unsigned. 1906. National Gallery of Art, Washington, D. C., Rosenwald Collection.

Compare K. 95.

29 MEN STORMING UP STEPS
BEWAFFNUNG IN EINEM GEWOELBE

Plate 4 of "Peasant War." Overpainted etching with light blue and white ink. 32.3 x 49.5 cm.; 12⅞ x 19½ in. Signed: Kollwitz. 1906. Collection: Gordon Fox, Montreal, Canada.

Corrected plate for the etching K. 95, first state.

30 RAPED WOMAN
VERGEWALTIGT

Study for plate 2 of "Peasant War." Pencil. 46.2 x 57.2 cm.; 18 x 22½ in. Signed: Kaethe Kollwitz. 1907. Galerie St. Etienne, New York.

Probably first sketch for K. 97. Reversed.

31 RAPED WOMAN
VERGEWALTIGT

Study for plate 2 of "Peasant War." Pencil on chamois paper. 39 x 59.2 cm.; 15½ x 23⅛ in. Signed: Kollwitz 07. 1907. Collection: Unknown. Richter Portfolio plate 8.

32 BATTLEFIELD
SCHLACHTFELD

Plate 6 from "Peasant War." Charcoal and pastel on dark gray paper. 45.7 x 55.9 cm.; 18 x 22 in. Signed: Kaethe Kollwitz. 1907. Collection: Gordon Fox, Montreal, Canada.

Drawing for the etching K. 96.

33 THE PRISONERS
DIE GEFANGENEN

Study for plate 7 of "Peasant War." Charcoal on brown paper. 27.9 x 43.2 cm.; 11 x 17 in. Signed: Kaethe Kollwitz. 1908 or earlier. Collection: Erich Cohn, New York.

Probably the first idea for the etching K. 98.

34 THE PRISONERS
DIE GEFANGENEN

Study for plate 7 of "Peasant War." Charcoal on white paper. 46.3 x 58.4 cm.; 18½ x 23 in. Signed: Kaethe Kollwitz. 1908. Collection: Mr. and Mrs. John Kallir, Scarsdale, N. Y.

Later version for the etching K. 98.

35 THE PRISONERS
DIE GEFANGENEN

Study for plate 7 of "Peasant War." Charcoal. 40.3 x 55.2 cm.; 15⅞ x 21¾ in. Signed: Kaethe Kollwitz. 1908. Formerly Private Collection, Dresden. Richter Portfolio plate 7.

Later version for K. 98, showing the artist's creative process, her way of *pentimenti,* and her ardent forward drive to achieve the final pictorial goal of her first idea. Compare the final etching, plate 36.

36 THE PRISONERS
DIE GEFANGENEN

Plate 7 of "Peasant War." Etching and soft ground. 32.7 x 42.3 cm.; 12⅞ x 16⅝ in. 1908. Collection: Erich Cohn, New York.

K. 98. State V.

37 FAREWELL
ABSCHIED

Charcoal on yellowish paper. 35 x 44.3 cm.; 13 9/16 x 17 1/16 in. Signed: Kollwitz 09. 1909. Collection: Unknown. Richter Portfolio plate 10.

38 MOTHER AT THE BED OF THE DEAD CHLD
MUTTER AM BETT DES TOTEN KINDES

Drawing for the *vernis-mou* (K. 117). Charcoal. 43 x 59.7 cm.; 16 15/16 x 23½ in. Signed: Kaethe Kollwitz. 1911. Collection: Unknown. Richter Portfolio plate 21.

39 SHEET WITH HEADS OF CHILDREN
BLATT MIT KINDERKOEPFEN

Pencil and crayon on yellowish paper. 45 x 59.3 cm.; 17¾ x 23 5/16 in. Signed: Kaethe Kollwitz. 1909. Formerly Kupferstichkabinett, Dresden. Richter Portfolio plate 14.

40 IN A PARIS TAVERN
IN EINER PARISER TAVERNE

Charcoal. 48.3 x 59.7 cm.; 19 x 23½ in. Signed and dated: Kaethe Kollwitz 1909. Collection: Mr. and Mrs. James S. Plant, Cambridge, Mass.

On the reverse: a family scene, unsigned.

41 MAN, MOTHERS, AND CHILDREN
MANN, MUETTER UND KINDER

Charcoal. 55.9 x 48.3 cm.; 22 x 19 in. Unsigned. 1909. Galerie St. Etienne, New York. Reverse of "In a Paris Tavern."

42 AT THE DOCTOR'S
BEIM ARZT

Drawing for "Simplicissimus." Charcoal on chamois paper. 59.7 x 45 cm.; 23½ x 17 9/16 in. Signed K. 1909. Collection: Unknown. Richter Portfolio plate 19.

43 WOMAN GOING INTO THE WATER
FRAU INS WASSER GEHEND

Charcoal on gray paper. 50.8 x 41.9 cm.; 20 x 16½ in. Signed: Kaethe Kollwitz. 1909. Collection: Erich Cohn, New York.

44 DRAWING FOR "SIMPLICISSIMUS"
ZEICHNUNG FUER DEN "SIMPLICISSIMUS"

Charcoal. Signed: Kollwitz. 1909. Erich Cohn, New York.

Early draft for "Bilder vom Elend," VI, *Simplicissimus.* Reversed. With *three* children.

45 DRAWING FOR "SIMPLICISSIMUS"
ZEICHNUNG FUER DEN "SIMPLICISSIMUS"

Charcoal. 56.8 x 44.6 cm.; 22⅜ x 17⅝ in. Signed: Kaethe Kollwitz. 1909. Formerly Private Collection, Dresden. Richter Portfolio plate 20.

Final draft for "Bilder vom Elend," VI, *Simplicissimus,* Vol. XIV, 1909, page 747. The third child has been omitted.

46 PETITION
BITTSTELLERIN

Charcoal. 31.1 x 52.1 cm.; 12¼ x 20½ in. Signed: Kollwitz. 1909. Collection: Joseph Katz, Baltimore, Maryland.

Published in *Simplicissimus,* 1909.

47 THE HOMELESS
DIE OBDACHLOSEN

Charcoal and wash, paper yellowed through earlier bad matting and framing. 45.7 x 52.8 cm.; 18 x 20¾ in. Signed: Kollwitz. 1909. National Gallery of Art, Washington, D. C., Rosenwald Collection.

Published 1909 in *Simplicissimus,* XIII, page 669, under the title "Die Jahreswende."

48 LUNCH HOUR
MITTAGSPAUSE

Pen, wash, and sepia on olive-green paper. 47 x 43.2 cm.; 18½ x 17 in. Signed: Kaethe Kollwitz. About 1909. Collection: Mr. and Mrs. William Lincer, New York.

49 UNEMPLOYMENT
ARBEITSLOSIGKEIT

Charcoal, pencil, white wash on gray-brown paper. 44.5 x 29.2 cm.; 17½ x 11½ in. Signed and dated: Kaethe Kollwitz, Arbeitslosigkeit, 1909. National Gallery of Art, Washington, D. C., Rosenwald Collection.

Published in *Simplicissimus,* XIV, i, page 267, under the title "Das einzige Glueck" (The Only Happiness). Study for the etching "Arbeitslosigkeit" (K. 100).

50 TWO STUDIES OF A WOMAN WITH KERCHIEF
ZWEI STUDIEN EINER FRAU MIT UMSCHLAGETUCH

Charcoal on gray paper. 61.6 x 47 cm.; 24¼ x 18½ in. Signed: Kaethe Kollwitz. 1909. Galerie St. Etienne, New York.

On the reverse: study of two nudes.

51 WOMAN WITH GOAT
FRAU MIT ZIEGE

Watercolor with crayon on brownish-gray paper. 30.4 x 22.9 cm.; 12 x 9 in.

Signed: Kaethe Kollwitz. About 1910. Collection: Erich Cohn, New York.

52 RUN OVER
UEBERFAHREN

Charcoal on brownish-yellow paper. 59 x 45 cm.; 23⅛ x 17¾ in. Signed: Kaethe Kollwitz. 1910. Collection: Unknown. Richter Portfolio plate 18.

Early study for the *vernis-mou* (K. 104).

53 RUN OVER
UEBERFAHREN

Charcoal on white paper. 27.3 x 43.2 cm.; 10¾ x 17 in. Signed: Kollwitz. 1910. Private Collection.

Drawing for K. 104.

54 SITTING NUDE
SITZENDER AKT

Charcoal. 42.2 x 47.6 cm.; 16⅝ x 18¾ in. Signed: K. About 1910. Collection: George Efron, New York.

55 NUDE
AKT

Charcoal. 62.9 x 47.6 cm.; 24¾ x 18¾ in. Signed: Kollwitz. About 1910. National Gallery of Art, Washington, D. C., Rosenwald Collection.

56 NUDE
AKT

Charcoal. 62.6 x 48.3 cm.; 24⅝ x 19 in. Signed: Kollwitz. About 1910. National Gallery of Art, Washington, D. C., Rosenwald Collection.

57 DEATH, WOMAN, AND CHILD
TOD, FRAU, UND KIND

Charcoal. 45.1 x 53.3 cm.; 17¾ x 21 in. Signed: Kaethe Kollwitz. 1910. Collection: Unknown. Richter Portfolio plate 11.

Study for K. 113.

58 DEATH, WOMAN, AND CHILD
TOD, FRAU, UND KIND

Charcoal on gray paper. 57.2 x 47 cm.; 22½ x 18½ in. Signed: Kaethe Kollwitz. 1910. Collection: Mr. and Mrs. Edgar Sinton, San Mateo, California.

Study for K. 113.

59 MOTHER AND CHILD
MUTTER UND KIND

Study for "Death, Mother, and Child" (K. 113). Charcoal. 62.9 x 47.9 cm.; 24¾ x 18⅞ in. Signed: Kaethe Kollwitz. 1910. National Gallery of Art, Washington, D. C., Rosenwald Collection.

From the estate of the artist.

60 FOUR PEOPLE SEATED ON A BENCH
VIER LEUTE AUF EINER BANK SITZEND

Pencil. 24.8 x 35.2 cm.; 9¾ x 13⅞ in. Signed and Dated: Kaethe Kollwitz (1912). National Gallery of Art. Washington, D. C., Rosenwald Collection.

61 WOMAN AND DEATH
TOD UND FRAU

Charcoal. 47 x 61 cm.; 18½ x 24 in. Signed and dated: K. 1910. National Gallery of Art, Washington, D. C., Rosenwald Collection.

First draft for the etching K. 103. Reversed.

62 PLAYING FORBIDDEN
SPIELEN VERBOTEN

Charcoal and wash. 71 x 50.6 cm.; 28 x 21 in. Signed and dated: Kollwitz 1912. Collection: Erich Cohn, New York.

Study for the poster, "Fuer Gross Berlin. Oeffentliche Versammlung am Sonntag den 10. Maerz 12 Uhr in der Brauerei Friedrichshain" (For Greater Berlin. Open Assembling on Sunday, March 10, 12 o'clock in the Brewery Friedrichshain). Reversed (K. 119, without the boy playing in the gully).

63 MOTHER WITH CHILD IN HER LAP
MUTTER MIT KIND IM SCHOSS

Crayon and pencil. 43 x 31.5 cm.; 17 x 12½ in. Signed: Kaethe Kollwitz. 1912. Collection: Gordon Fox, Montreal, Canada.

Drawing for the *vernis-mou* (K. 120).

64 MOURNING THE DEAD OF 1848
MAERZFRIEDHOF

Charcoal. 54.7 x 47 cm.; 21½ x 18½ in. Signed: Kaethe Kollwitz. 1913. Collection: Erich Cohn, New York.

Drawing for K. 125, third state.

65 SELF PORTRAIT
SELBSTBILDNIS

Charcoal on brownish-yellow paper. 35.5 x 30.5 cm.; 14 x 12 in. Signed and dated: Kaethe Kollwitz 1916. Collection: Unknown. Richter Portfolio plate 1.

66 WOMAN WITH CHILD IN HER LAP
FRAU MIT KIND IM SCHOSS

Charcoal. 54.7 x 67.3 cm.; 21½ x 26½ in. Signed: Kaethe Kollwitz. 1916. Collection Erich Cohn, New York. Richter Portfolio.

67 FRIGHTENED MOTHER AND CHILD
VERAENGSTIGTE MUTTER MIT KIND

Charcoal on gray paper. 35.6 x 25.4 cm.; 14 x 10 in. Signed: Kollwitz. About 1916. Collection: Dr. and Mrs. Otto Kallir, New York.

68 ANGUISH. THE WIDOW
ANGST. DIE WITWE

Charcoal on brown paper. 48.2 x 35.6 cm.; 19 x 14 in. Signed: Kollwitz. 1916. Collection: Erich Cohn, New York.

Drawing for the *vernis-mou* "The Widow," second version (K. 131).

69 CONTEMPLATION
NACHDENKEN

Charcoal and pencil. 39.4 x 22.3 cm.; 15½ x 18¾ in. Signed: Kaethe Kollwitz. 1918. Collection: Mr. and Mrs. Moses Soyer, New York.

Illustration for Heinrich Mann's novel, *The Poor*.

70 MEDITATING WOMAN
NACHDENKENDE FRAU

Charcoal. 27.3 x 38.1 cm.; 10¾ x 15 in. Signed: Kaethe Kollwitz. About 1918. Collection: Mr. and Mrs. James Lipton, New York.

71 THE MOTHERS
DIE MUETTER

Charcoal. 46.7 x 31.8 cm.; 18⅜ x 12½

in. Signed: Kaethe Kollwitz. 1919. National Gallery of Art, Washington, D. C., Rosenwald Collection.

First idea for "The Mothers" (K. 134, etching, and K. 135, lithograph).

72 MOTHERS PROTECTING THEIR CHILDREN
MUETTER IHRE KINDER BESCHIRMEND

Charcoal on gray paper. 45.1 x 61 cm.; 17¾ x 24 in. Signed and dated: Kollwitz 1918 Muetter ihre Kinder beschirmend. Private Collection.

Drawing for K. 134, 1919.

73 WOMAN WEEPING
WEINENDE FRAU

Charcoal on blue paper. 47.6 x 32.7 cm.; 18¾ x 12⅝ in. Signed: Kaethe Kollwitz weinende Frau. 1918. National Gallery of Art, Washington, D. C., Rosenwald Collection.

74 SKETCH FOR THE MEMORIAL TO KARL LIEBKNECHT
SKIZZE FUER DAS GEDENKBLATT FUER KARL LIEBKNECHT

Pencil on gray-green paper. 41.9 x 61.6 cm.; 16½ x 24½ in. Unsigned. 1919. Collection: Erich Cohn, New York.

First draft for the "Gedenkblatt" (K. 137, 138, and 139), executed later as etching, lithograph, and woodcut. On the bottom: "Aus dem Nachlass meiner Mutter Kaethe Kollwitz erworben am 4. Juni 50 durch Herrn Erich Cohn. Hans Kollwitz."

75 COLLECTING COAL
KOHLENSAMMLER

Pen on gray paper. 31.1 x 48.6 cm.; 12¼ x 19⅛ in. Signed: Kaethe Kollwitz. About 1920. Collection: Gordon Fox, Montreal, Canada.

76 HEAD AND HANDS OF A WORKING MAN
KOPF UND HAENDE EINES ARBEITERS

Charcoal on gray paper. 65.1 x 50.2 cm.; 25⅝ x 19¾ in. Signed: Kaethe Kollwitz. About 1920. National Gallery of Art, Washington D. C., Rosenwald Collection.

77 WOMAN IN SICKBED
FRAU IM KRANKENBETT

Charcoal. 49.5 x 40.6 cm.; 19½ x 16 in. Signed: Kaethe Kollwitz. About 1920. Collection: Erich Cohn, New York.

78 MOTHER LEADING TWO CHILDREN
MUTTER ZWEI KINDER FUEHREND

Charcoal. 48.2 x 31.8 cm.; 19 x 12½ in. Signed: Kaethe Kollwitz. About 1920. Collection: Herman H. Stone, Scarsdale, New York.

79 WOMAN THINKING
NACHDENKENDE FRAU

Charcoal and pencil. 48.3 x 35.6 cm.; 19 x 14 in. Signed: Kaethe Kollwitz. 1920. Collection: Erich Cohn, New York.

80 STUDIES FOR "IN THE WAITING ROOM OF THE CHILDREN'S DOCTOR"
STUDIEN ZU "IN DER SPRECHSTUNDE DES KINDERARZTES"

Wash, charcoal, and pencil. 40.6 x 62.3 cm.; 16 x 24½ in. Signed twice: Kaethe

Kollwitz. 1920. Collection: Erich Cohn, New York.

Studies for the three leaflets "Against Usury" (K. 148-50).

81 STUDIES FOR "IN THE WAITING ROOM OF THE CHILDREN'S DOCTOR"
STUDIEN ZU "IN DER SPRECHSTUNDE DES KINDERARZTES"

Pen. Signed: Kollwitz. 1920. Collection: Erich Cohn, New York.

82 WOMAN CARESSING CHILD
FRAU KIND LIEBKOSEND

Charcoal on grayish paper. 51.2 x 45.1 cm.; 20⅛ x 17¾ in. Signed: Kaethe Kollwitz. About 1920. Kunsthalle, Mannheim, Germany. Richter Portfolio plate 13.

83 STUDIES OF A SLEEPING CHILD
STUDIEN EINES SCHLAFENDEN KINDES

Charcoal. 48.9 x 63.3 cm.; 19¼ x 24⅞ in. Signed: Kaethe Kollwitz. About 1920. New Art Center Gallery, New York.

84 STUDIES OF A BABY'S HEAD
STUDIE EINES KINDERKOPFES

Charcoal on cream paper. 25.4 x 29.2 cm.; 10 x 11½ in. Signed: Kaethe Kollwitz. About 1921. Baltimore Museum of Art, Museum Purchase.

85 DOUBLE PORTRAIT
DOPPELPORTRAET

Chalk on cream paper. 34.3 x 55.9 cm.; 13½ x 22 in. Signed and dated: Kaethe Kollwitz 1921. Baltimore Museum of Art, Gift of W. A. Dickey, Jr.

86 DEATH WITH WOMAN IN LAP
TOD MIT FRAU IM SCHOSS

Charcoal. 34.3 x 36.8 cm.; 13½ x 14½ in. Signed and dated: Kaethe Kollwitz. 1921. Collection: Erich Cohn, New York.

Study for the woodcut K. 151.

87 THE PARENTS
DIE ELTERN

Charcoal. 42.3 x 55.8 cm.; 16 7/16 x 22 in. Signed and dated: Kaethe Kollwitz. 1920. Collection: Unknown. Richter Portfolio plate 24.

Drawing for the lithograph K. 144. Kaethe Kollwitz made this drawing for "War."

88 THE WIDOW
DIE WITWE

Charcoal. 57.2 x 38.7 cm.; 21½ x 15¼ in. Signed: Kaethe Kollwitz. 1922-23. Collection: Mr. and Mrs. Edgar Sinton, San Mateo, California.

First draft for plate 4 of "War." Compare with K. 180.

89 THE VOLUNTEERS
DIE FREIWILLIGEN

Wash and Chinese white. 33 x 52.1 cm.; 13 x 20½ in. Signed: Kaethe Kollwitz, Die Freiwilligen. 1922. Collection: Erich Cohn, New York.

Drawing for the woodcut "Die Freiwilligen," plate 2 of "War." Compare with K. 178.

90 THE WIDOW
DIE WITWE

Black ink and Chinese white. 36.8 x 26.7 cm.; 14½ x 10½ in. Signed: Kaethe Kollwitz, Zeichnung zu "Witwe" Folge Krieg. 1922-23. Collection: Erich Cohn, New York.

Drawing for plate 4 of "War" (K. 180).

91 THE MOTHERS
DIE MUETTER

Ink and Chinese white. 45.7 x 59.1 cm.; 18 x 23¼ in. Signed: Kaethe Kollwitz. Zeichnung zu den Muettern. 1922-23. Museum of Fine Arts, Boston.

Drawing for plate 6 (K. 182) of "War."

92 THE PEOPLE
DAS VOLK

Black and white ink, charcoal. 43.8 x 52.7 cm.; 17¼ x 20¾ in. Signed: Kaethe Kollwitz. 1922-23. Collection: Gordon Fox, Montreal.

Study for plate 7 (K. 183) of "War." On the reverse: Charcoal sketch of girl carrying child. Mat bears description in artist's handwriting:"Kaethe Kollwitz. Berlin. Zeichnung zur Folge Krieg—das Volk. Preis ~~100~~ 400 Goldmark." The correction is due to the inflation in Germany.

93 SKETCH FOR "KILLED IN ACTION"
ERSTE ZEICHNUNG FUER "GEFALLEN"

Charcoal. Signed: Kaethe Kollwitz. 1921. Collection: Erich Cohn, New York.

Compare with K. 152 and 153.

94 KILLED IN ACTION
GEFALLEN

Crayon and pencil on off-white smooth pulp paper. 48.2 x 42.2 cm.; 19 x 16⅝ in. Signed: Kaethe Kollwitz Gefallen. 1921. Baltimore Museum of Art, Gift of Mr. and Mrs. Albert Lion.

On the reverse: figure of a woman. Black crayon.

95 THE SURVIVORS
DIE UEBERLEBENDEN

Charcoal. 62.9 x 48 cm.; 24¾ x 18⅞ in. Signed: Kaethe Kollwitz. 1923. National Gallery of Art, Washington, D. C., Rosenwald Collection.

First draft for the lithograph K. 184. Poster for the "Internationale Gewerkschaftsbund," Amsterdam.

96 THE SURVIVORS
DIE UEBERLEBENDEN

Charcoal. 49.5 x 64.8 cm.; 19½ x 25½ in. Signed: Kaethe Kollwitz. 1923. Collection: Dr. and Mrs. Otto Kallir, New York.

Later draft for the lithograph K. 184.

97 DEATH REACHES FOR A WOMAN
TOD PACKT EINE FRAU

Charcoal. 49.4 x 37.4 cm.; 19½ x 14¾ in. Unsigned. 1924. Collection: Unknown.

Drawing for the lithograph K. 259. published 1934. Reproduced in the portfolio *Abschied und Tod,* with a preface by Gerhart Hauptmann, 1924.

98 DEATH GIVING COMFORT
TOD TROESTEND

Charcoal on greenish paper. 49.4 x 37.4 cm.; 19½ x 14¾ in. Unsigned. 1923-24. Collection: Unknown.

Drawing for the portfolio *Abschied und Tod,* with a preface by Gerhart Hauptmann.

99 SKETCH FOR THE POSTER "HEIMARBEIT"
ENTWURF FUER DAS PLAKAT "HEIMARBEIT"

Lithograph crayon. 31.7 x 35.6 cm.; 12½ x 14 in. Signed: Kollwitz. 1924. Collection: Erich Cohn, New York.

Published as poster for the "'Homeworker" Exhibition of the Unions.

100 WOMAN WITH CHILDREN GOING TO THEIR DEATH
FRAU MIT KINDERN IN DEN TOD GEHEND

Charcoal on gray paper. 50.8 x 43.2 cm.; 20 x 17 in. Signed: Kaethe Kollwitz. 1924. Galerie St. Etienne, New York.

Drawing for the woodcut K. 188.

101 MOTHER AND SICK CHILD
MUTTER UND KRANKES KIND

Black and white Chinese ink. 52.1 x 48.2 cm.; 20½ x 19 in. Signed: Kollwitz. About 1924. Collection: Mrs. Howard G. Kornblith, Chicago, Illinois.

102 SITTING WOMAN WITH THE HAND OF DEATH
SITZENDE FRAU MIT DER HAND DES TODES

Self portrait. Charcoal. 60.4 x 47.8 cm.; 23 3/16 x 18 3/16 in. Signed and dated in pencil: Kaethe Kollwitz 1924. Allen Memorial Art Museum, Oberlin College, Oberlin, Ohio.

Early study for the lithograph K. 192.

103 BEGGARS
BETTELNDE

Charcoal. 38.1 x 28.6 cm.; 15 x 11¼ in. Signed: Kaethe Kollwitz. 1924. National Gallery of Art, Washington, D. C., Rosenwald Collection.

Transfer drawing for the lithograph K. 193.

104 STUDY FOR "GERMANY'S CHILDREN STARVING" (EMPTY DISHES)
STUDIE FUER "DEUTSCHLANDS KINDER HUNGERN" (LEERE TELLER)

Charcoal and pencil. 41.9 x 36.8 cm.; 16½ x 14½ in. Signed and dated: Kaethe Kollwitz 1924. Galerie St. Etienne, New York.

K. 190.

105 BREAD!
BROT!

Charcoal on white paper. 80 x 31 cm.; 31½ x 12 in. Signed: Kaethe Kollwitz. 1924. Collection: Erich Cohn, New York.

Transfer drawing for the lithograph K. 196.

106 SELF PORTRAIT
SELBSTBILDNIS

Charcoal and pencil. 36.8 x 29.2 cm.;

14½ x 11½ in. Signed: Kollwitz, Litho-zeichnung. 1924. National Gallery of Art, Washington, D. C., Rosenwald Collection.

Transfer drawing for the lithograph K. 198.

107 NEVER AGAIN WAR
NIE WIEDER KRIEG

Charcoal on two pieces of paper glued together. 98.9 x 75 cm.; 38¾ x 29½ in. Signed: Kaethe Kollwitz (and) Kollwitz. 1924. National Gallery of Art, Washington, D. C., Rosenwald Collection.

Drawing for K. 200.

108 UNEMPLOYED
ERWERBSLOS

Charcoal on brownish paper. 41.9 x 27.9 cm.; 16½ x 11 in. Signed: Kaethe Kollwitz, Erwerbslos. 1925. Collection: Erich Cohn, New York. Richter Portfolio.

109 SELF PORTRAIT
SELBSTBILDNIS

Charcoal. 30.4 x 33 cm.; 12 x 13 in. Signed: Kaethe Kollwitz, Selbsbild. About 1925. Collection: Erich Cohn, New York.

110 CHILD'S HEAD (LOTTE)
KINDERKOPF (LOTTE)

Crayon, transfer drawing. Approximately 20.9 x 14.6 cm.; 8¼ x 5¾ in. Irregularly cut from a larger piece of paper. Signed: Kollwitz. 1925. National Gallery of Art, Washington, D. C., Rosenwald Collection.

Transfer drawing for the lithograph K. 213.

111 TWO CHILDREN
ZWEI KINDER

Crayon on chamois paper. 24.2 x 30.5 cm.; 9½ x 12 in. Signed twice: Kaethe Kollwitz. About 1925. New Art Center Gallery, New York.

The drawing was in a frame for some time; after the mat was removed, deep staining was left on the left and lower margin, which may explain the duplication of the signature.

112 FIGURE OF A YOUNG GIRL
KIND

Charcoal on off-white smooth pulp paper, probably a sketch-book sheet. 48.3 x 38.1 cm.; 19 x 15 in. Unsigned. 1925. Baltimore Museum of Art, Blanche Adler Purchase Fund.

On the reverse: a drawing, "The Demonstration."

113 PRISONERS LISTENING TO MUSIC
GEFANGENE, MUSIK HOEREND

Charcoal. Approximately 43.8 x 36.8 cm.; 17¼ x 14½ in. Irregularly cut. Unsigned. 1925. National Gallery of Art, Washington, D. C., Rosenwald Collection.

Transfer drawing for K. 203. Penciled caption "original Litho-zeichnung" may not be by the artist.

114 TWO HEADS
ZWEI KOEPFE

Charcoal. 44.1 x 62.9 cm.; 17⅜ x 24¾ in. Signed: Kollwitz. National Gallery of Art, Washington, D. C., Rosenwald Collection.

115 PORTRAIT OF A YOUNG MAN
PORTRAET EINES JUNGEN MANNES

Charcoal. 67 x 52.1 cm.; 26 3/8 x 20 1/2 in. Signed: Kaethe Kollwitz. National Gallery of Art, Washington, D. C., Rosenwald Collection.

116 TWO NUDES
ZWEI AKTE

Charcoal. 61 x 48.2 cm.; 24 x 19 in. Signed: Kollwitz. National Gallery of Art, Washington, D. C., Rosenwald Collection.

117 WORKING WOMAN AND SLEEPING BOY
ARBEITERFRAU UND SCHLAFENDER JUNGE

Charcoal. 36.8 x 31.7 cm.; 14 1/2 x 12 1/2 in. Unsigned. 1927. Collection: Erich Cohn, New York.

Drawing for the lithograph K. 226.

118 MARIA AND ELIZABETH
MARIA UND ELISABETH

Grease crayon. 54 x 46.9 cm.; 21 1/4 x 19 7/16 in. Signed: Kaethe Kollwitz (Fettkreide). 1928. Collection: Erich Cohn, New York.

Drawing for K. 234, third version. Reversed.

119 SLEEPING BOY
SCHLAFENDER JUNGE

Charcoal. Approximately 30 1/2 x 37 cm.; 12 x 14 1/2 in. Signed and dated: Kaethe Kollwitz 1930. Collection: Mrs. Paul Keefe, New York.

120 SLEEPING CHILD
SCHLAFENDES KIND

Pencil. 43.2 x 31.8 cm.; 17 x 12 1/2 in. Signed: Kollwitz. About 1930. New Art Center Gallery, New York.

121 SLEEPING CHILD
SCHLAFENDES KIND

Charcoal. 62.2 x 48.2 cm.; 24 1/2 x 19 in. Signed: Kollwitz. About 1930. National Gallery of Art, Washington D. C., Rosenwald Collection.

122 DRAFT FOR ROGGEVELDE
ENTWURF FUER ROGGEVELDE

Charcoal. 48.2 x 39.3 cm.; 19 x 15 1/2 in. Unsigned. 1930. Collection: Erich Cohn, New York.

123 DRAFT FOR ROGGEVELDE
ENTWURF FUER ROGGEVELDE

Charcoal. 45.7 x 43.2 cm.; 18 x 17 in. Unsigned. 1930. Collection: Erich Cohn, New York.

On the bottom: "Aus dem Nachlass meiner Mutter Kaethe Kollwitz erworben von Herrn Erich Cohn 4. Juni 1950. Hans Kollwitz."

124 MOTHER AND CHILD
MUTTER UND KIND

Pen and wash. 42.6 x 27.3 cm.; 16 3/4 x 10 1/4 in. Signed: Kaethe Kollwitz. 1931. National Gallery of Art, Washington, D. C., Rosenwald Collection.

Early study for the lithograph "Young Mother with Child on the Arm" (K. 245).

125 MOTHER WITH BOY
MUTTER MIT JUNGEN

Charcoal. 49.5 x 27.9 cm.; 19 1/2 x 11

in. Signed: Kaethe Kollwitz. 1931. Collection: Erich Cohn, New York.

Drawing for lithograph K. 246.

126 MOTHER WITH CHILDREN
MUTTER MIT KINDERN

Charcoal. 64.4 x 48.3 cm.; 25 3/8 x 19 in. Signed: Kaethe Kollwitz. 1932. Collection: Erich Cohn, New York.

127 MOTHER WITH CHILDREN
MUTTER MIT KINDERN

Charcoal. Signed and dated: Kaethe Kollwitz 1932. Collection: Mrs. Rebecca Schulman, Hadassah, New York.

128 SITTING WOMAN
SITZENDE FRAU

Charcoal. 59 x 42 cm.; 23 1/4 x 16 9/16 in. Signed: Kollwitz. About 1930. Collection: Erich Cohn, New York.

129 TWO WOMEN
ZWEI FRAUEN

Charcoal. 46 x 45.5 cm.; 18 1/8 x 17 1/8 in. Signed: Kollwitz. About 1930. Collection: Erich Cohn, New York.

130 MOTHER AND CHILD
MUTTER UND KIND

Charcoal. 35.6 x 33 cm.; 14 x 13 in. Signed: Kaethe Kollwitz. About 1931. Baltimore Museum of Art, Blanche Adler Purchase Fund.

131 PARENTS AND SICK CHILD
ELTERN UND KRANKES KIND

Charcoal. 57.5 x 44.2 cm.; 22 5/8 x 17 3/8 in. About 1930. Collection: Dr. and Mrs. A. Glaser, Troy, N. Y.

132 OLD COUPLE
ALTES PAAR

Charcoal. 38.1 x 24.2 cm.; 15 x 9 1/2 in. Signed: Kollwitz. About 1932. Collection: Erich Cohn, New York.

133 MOTHER AND CHILD
MUTTER UND KIND

Charcoal. 47 x 26.7 cm.; 18 1/2 x 10 1/2 in. Signed: Kaethe Kollwitz. About 1932. Collection: Erich Cohn, New York.

134 ALCOHOL
ALKOHOL

Charcoal on gray paper. 51 x 41.9 cm.; 20 x 16 1/2 in. Signed: Kaethe Kollwitz. About 1932. Collection: Erich Cohn, New York.

135 OLD COUPLE
ALTES PAAR

Charcoal on gray paper. 40.7 x 43.2 cm.; 16 x 17 in. Signed: Kaethe Kollwitz. About 1932. Collection: Erich Cohn, New York.

136 SELF PORTRAIT
SELBSTBILDNIS

Charcoal. 47.6 x 63.5 cm.; 18 3/4 x 25 in. Signed and dated: Kaethe Kollwitz 1933. National Gallery of Art, Washington, D. C., Rosenwald Collection.

137 SELF PORTRAIT
SELBSTBILDNIS

Charcoal. 55.9 x 44.4 cm.; 22 x 17 1/2 in. Signed and dated: Kaethe Kollwitz 1934. Collection: Erich Cohn, New York.

138 DRAWING OF THE WRITER WILHELMINE MOHR
ZEICHNUNG DER SCHRIFTSTELLERIN WILHELMINE MOHR

Charcoal. 44.4 x 33.7 cm.; 17½ x 13¼ in. Signed and dated: Kaethe Kollwitz 1933. Zeichnung der Schriftstellerin Wilhelmine Mohr. National Gallery of Art, Washington, D. C. Rosenwald Collection.

139 SITTING WOMAN
SITZENDE FRAU

Charcoal. 64.8 x 48.2 cm.; 25½ x 19 in. Signed with pencil: Kaethe Kollwitz, Sitzende Frau. National Gallery of Art, Washington, D. C., Rosenwald Collection.

140 WOMAN WELCOMING DEATH
FRAU HEISST DEN TOD WILLKOMMEN

Charcoal. 48.2 x 43.2 cm.; 19 x 17 in. Signed and dated: Kaethe Kollwitz, 1934. Collection: Erich Cohn, New York.

Variant study for the lithograph of "Death," plate 1 (K. 256).

141 THE HAND OF DEATH
FRAU REICHT DEM TODE DIE HAND

Charcoal on yellowish paper. 58.9 x 48.2 cm.; 23 x 19 in. Signed and dated: Kaethe Kollwitz, 1934. Collection: Erich Cohn, New York.

Rejected drawing for "Death" (K. 256-63).

142 MOURNING FIGURE: STUDY FOR "DEATH"
ZEICHNUNG ZUR FOLGE TOD

Charcoal on light gray paper. 55.2 x 43.2 cm.; 21¾ x 17 in. Signed and dated: Kaethe Kollwitz 1934, Zeichnung zur Folge Tod gehoerig. Baltimore Museum of Art, Museum Purchase.

Sketch belonging in "Death" (K. 256-63). It was ultimately rejected.

143 FETTERED MAN
GEFESSELTER

Pen and wash. 44.5 x 36.8 cm.; 17½ x 14½ in. Signed: Kollwitz. 1927. Collection: Erich Cohn, New York.

144 MOTHER AND TWO CHILDREN (STANDING)
MUTTER MIT ZWEI KINDERN (STEHEND)

Charcoal. 60 x 45.8 cm.; 23⅝ x 18 in. Signed: Kaethe Kollwitz. About 1934. Collection: Mr. and Mrs. Abe Lerner, Brooklyn, N. Y.

Probably study for "Woman giving herself up to Death" (K. 256). There are two *pentimenti:* One is just to the left of the taller child's head; the other is below the first. Both show the mother's right hand extended to the left, apparently in a gesture of begging.

On the reverse: Four light sketches. Three are of a mother holding a sleeping baby on her lap; the fourth is a head of a little girl in profile to the right. Charcoal.

145 MOTHER AND BABIES
MUTTER UND KINDER

Charcoal and pencil. 38.1 x 34.3 cm.; 15 x 13½ in. Signed: Kollwitz. 1928. Collection: Gordon Fox, Montreal.

146 DEATH REACHES INTO A GROUP OF CHILDREN
TOD GREIFT IN EINE KINDERSCHAR

Charcoal. 70 x 52.5 cm.; 27 9/16 x 20⅝ in. Signed: Kaethe Kollwitz. 1934. Collection: Erich Cohn, New York.

Sketch for the lithograph K. 258, plate 3 of "Death."

147 SELF PORTRAIT IN PROFILE TO THE RIGHT
SELBSTBILDNIS IM PROFIL NACH RECHTS

Lithograph with corrections by the hand of the artist. 49 x 30 cm.; 19 1/16 x 19 9/16 in. Signed. 1938. National Gallery of Art, Washington, D. C., Rosenwald Collection.

Early state of K. 265 with voluminous additions made by the hand of the artist in wash on forehead, chin, ear, and eyes. Spatters to the right and bottom.

Study of a Man

2 Self Portrait at the Table with Her Future Husband, Dr. Karl Kollwitz

3 Kaethe Kollwitz with Son, Hans

4 Interior for "The Weavers"

5 Six Men at the Table

6 Death

7 Storm

8 Marching Weavers

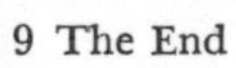

9 The End

10 Study of a Woman for "Downtrodden"

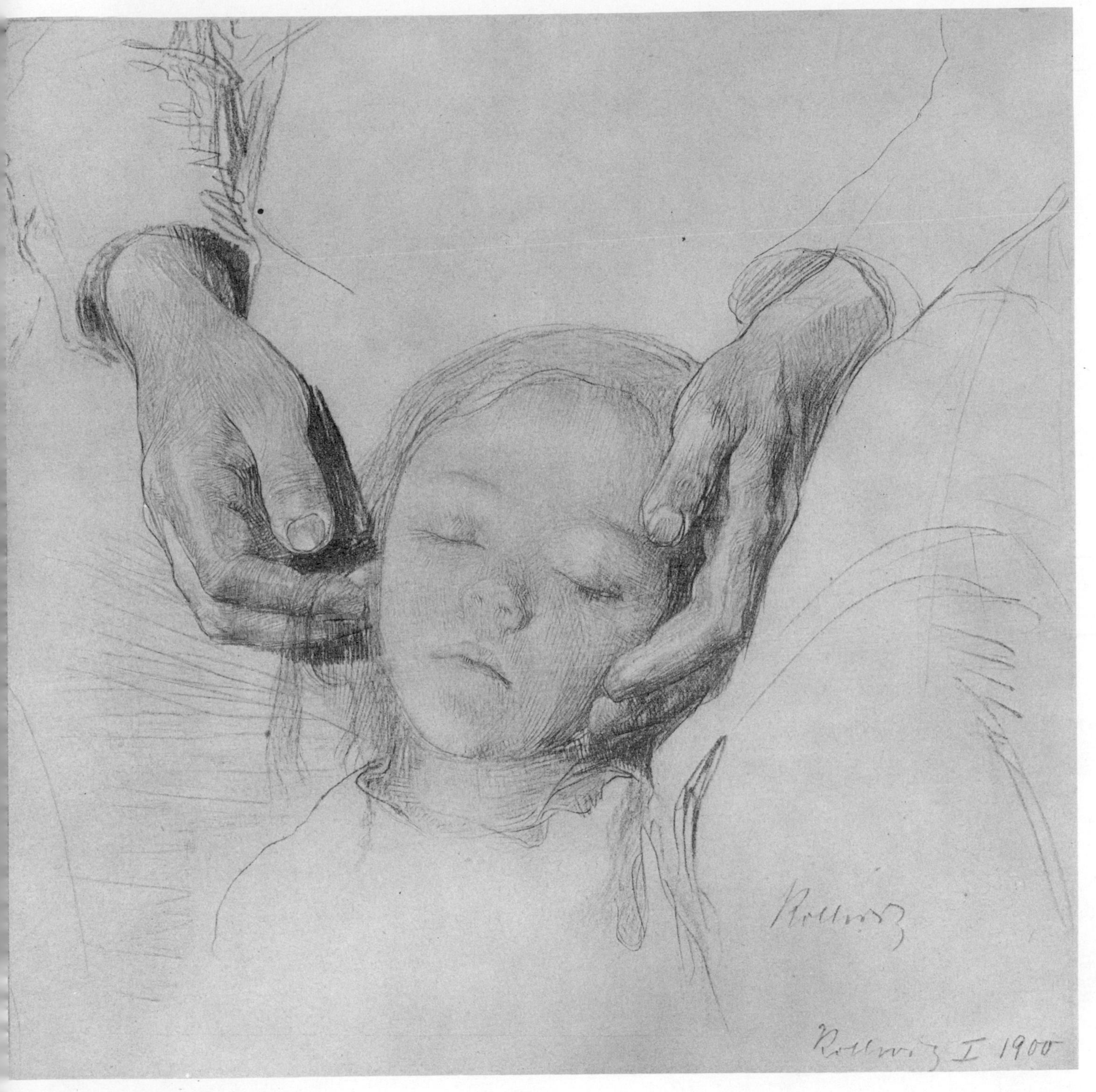


11 Study of a Child for "Downtrodden"

12 Gretchen

13 Woman Peeling Potatoes

14 Scolding Mother

15 Mother with Two Children

16 The Carmagnole (Dance Around the Guillotine)

17 The Carmagnole (Dance Around the Guillotine)

18 Study for the Carmagnole

19 Drummer Boy

20 Pietà

21 Mother with Dead Child

22 Outbreak

23 Standing Woman

24 Woman with Scythe

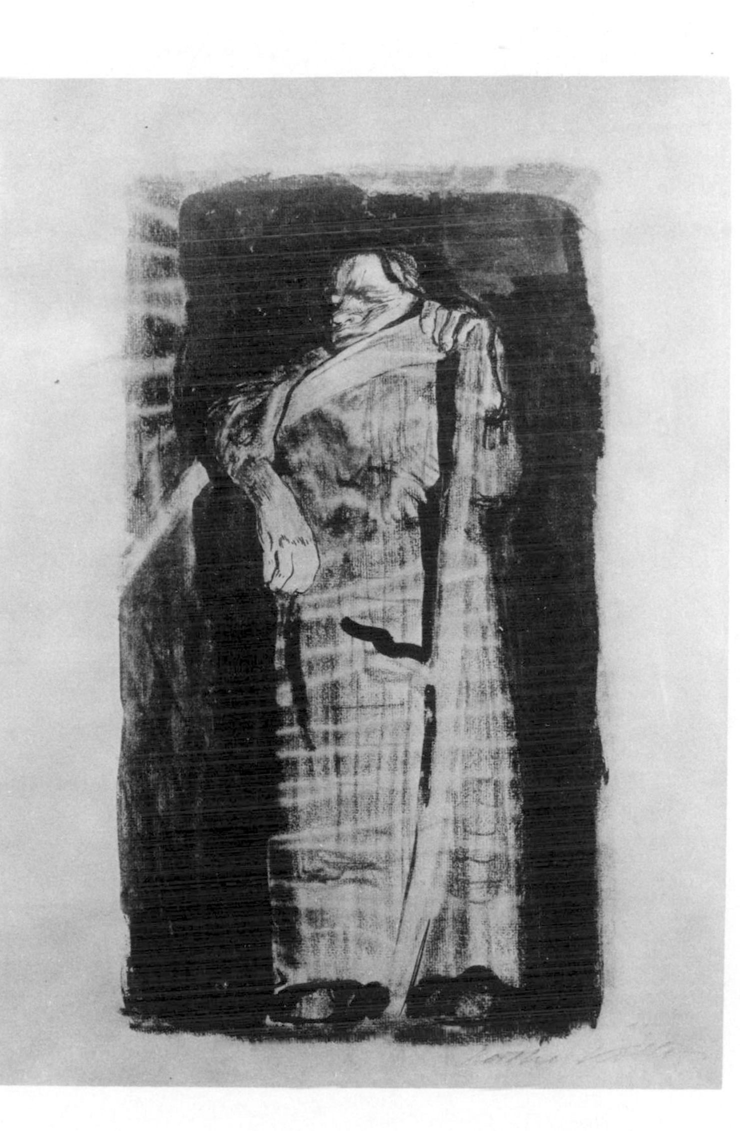

25 Woman with Scythe

26 Woman on the Bench

27 Home Worker

28 Men Storming Up Steps

29 Men Storming Up Steps

30 Raped Woman

31 Raped Woman

32 Battlefield

33 The Prisoners

34 The Prisoners

35 The Prisoners

36 The Prisoners (Etching)

37 Farewell

38 Mother at the Bed of the Dead Child

39 Sheet with Heads of Children

40 In a Paris Tavern

41 Man, Mothers, and Children

42 At the Doctor's

Woman Going into the Water

44 Drawing for "Simplicissimus"

45 Drawing for "Simplicissimus"

46 Petition

47 The Homeless

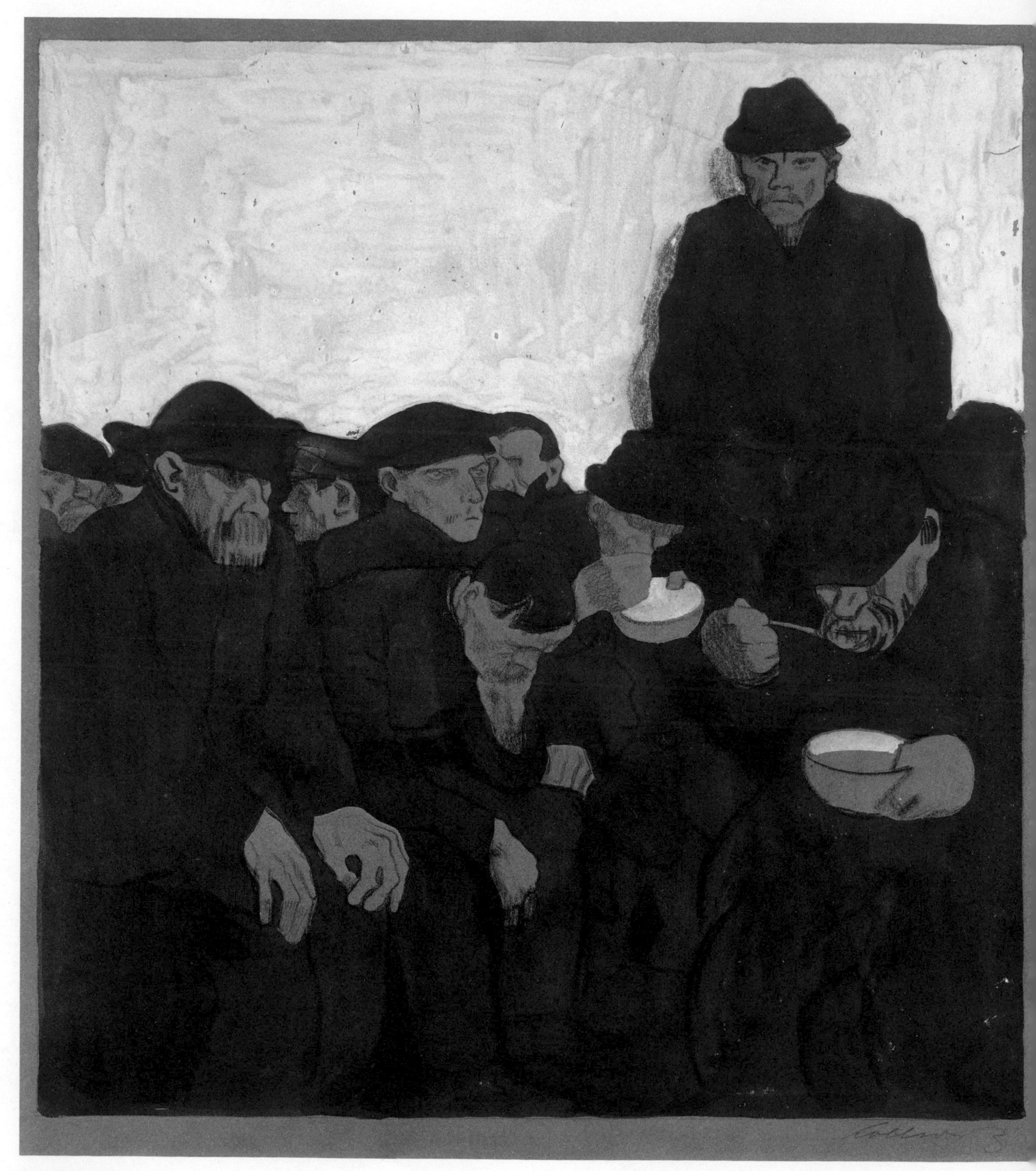

48 Lunch Hour

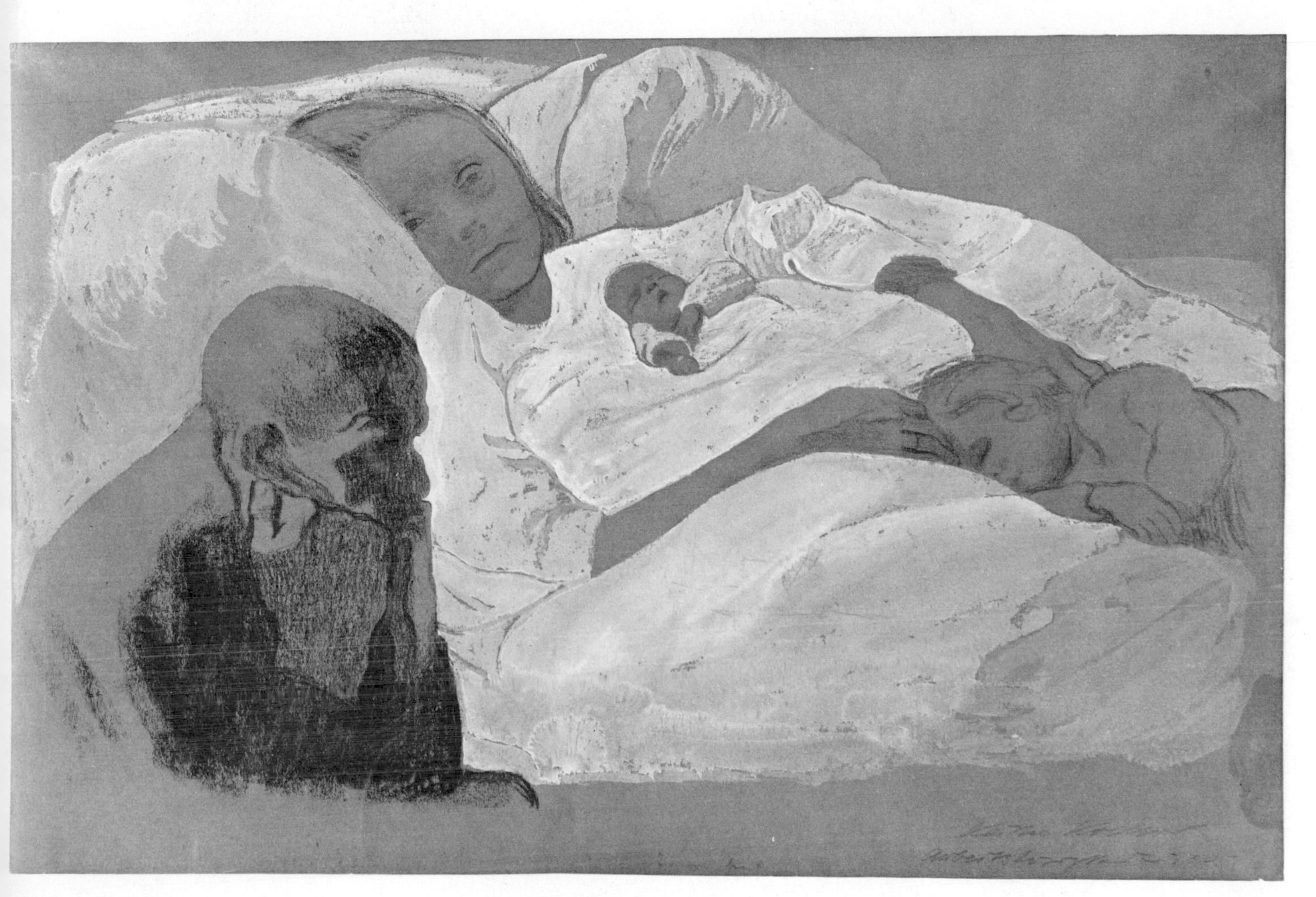

49 Unemployment

50 Two Studies of a Woman with Kerchief

51 Woman with Goat

52 Run Over

3 Run Over

54 Sitting Nude

55 Nude

56 Nude

57 Death, Woman, and Child

58 Death, Woman, and Child

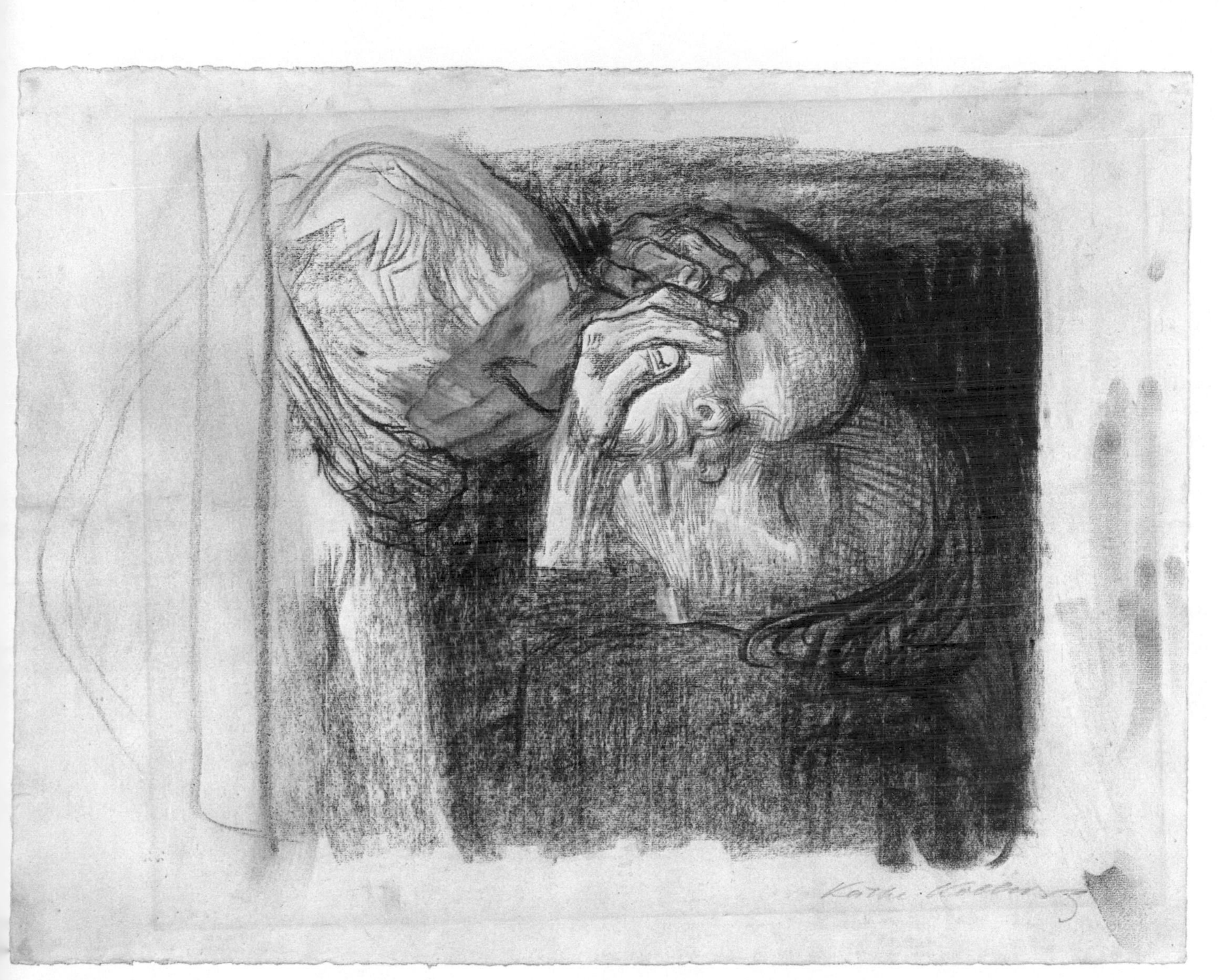

59 Mother and Child

60 Four People Seated on a Bench

61 Woman and Death

62 Playing Forbidden

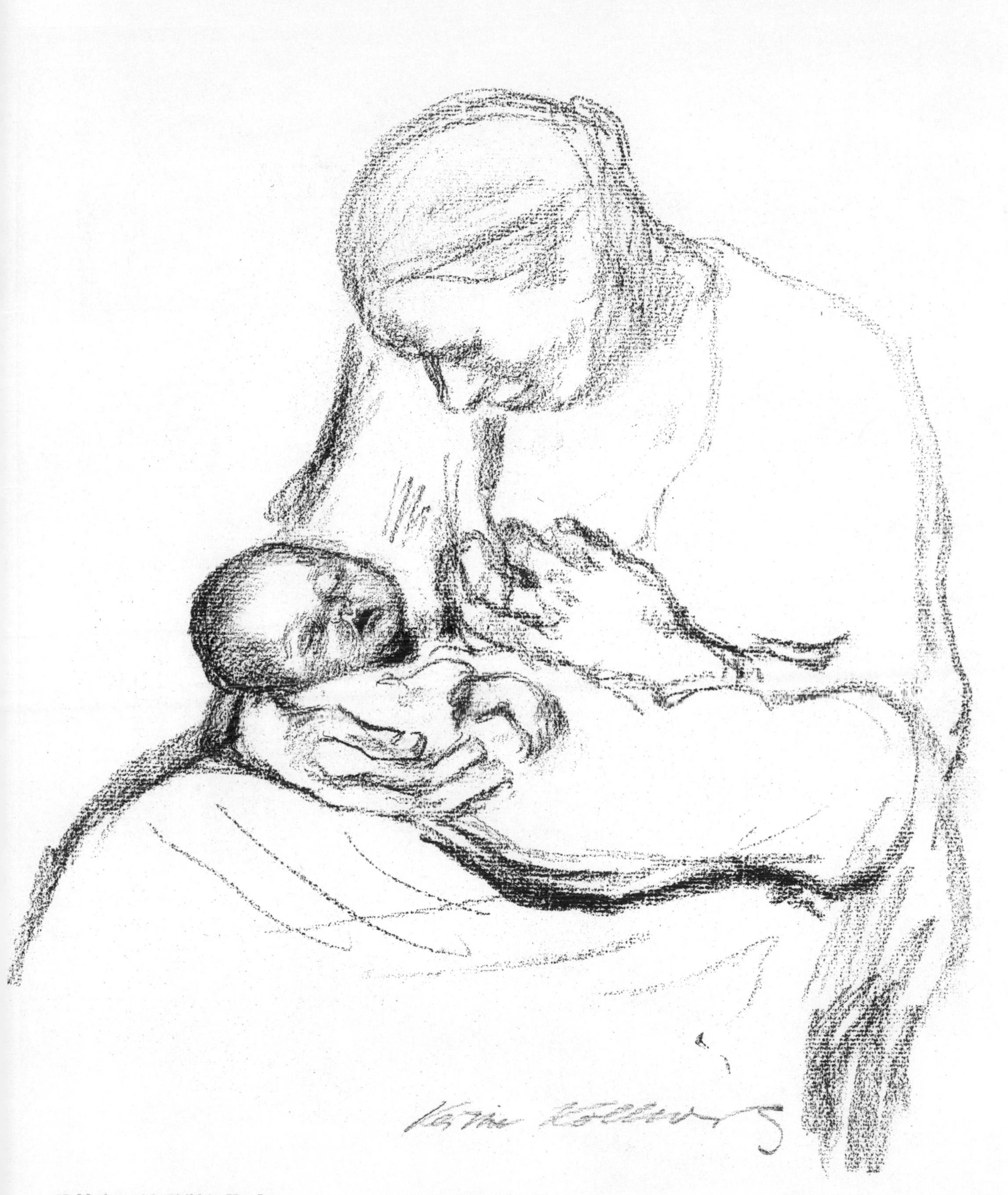

63 Mother with Child in Her Lap

64 Mourning the Dead of 1848

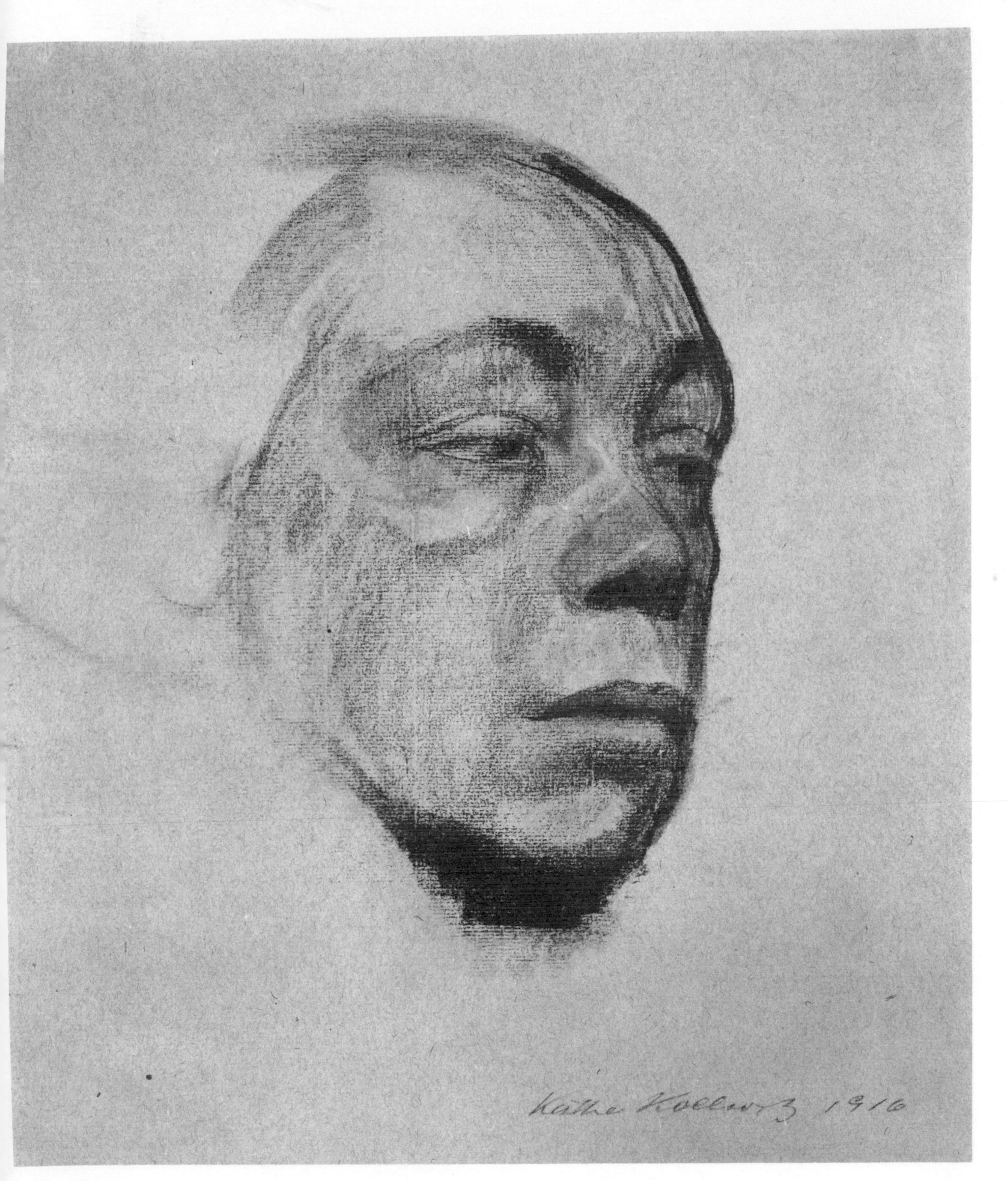


65 Self Portrait

66 Woman with Child in Her Lap

67 Frightened Mother and Child

68 Anguish. The Widow

69 Contemplation

70 Meditating Woman

71 The Mothers

72 Mothers Protecting Their Children

73 Woman Weeping

74 Sketch for the Memorial to Karl Liebknecht

75 Collecting Coal

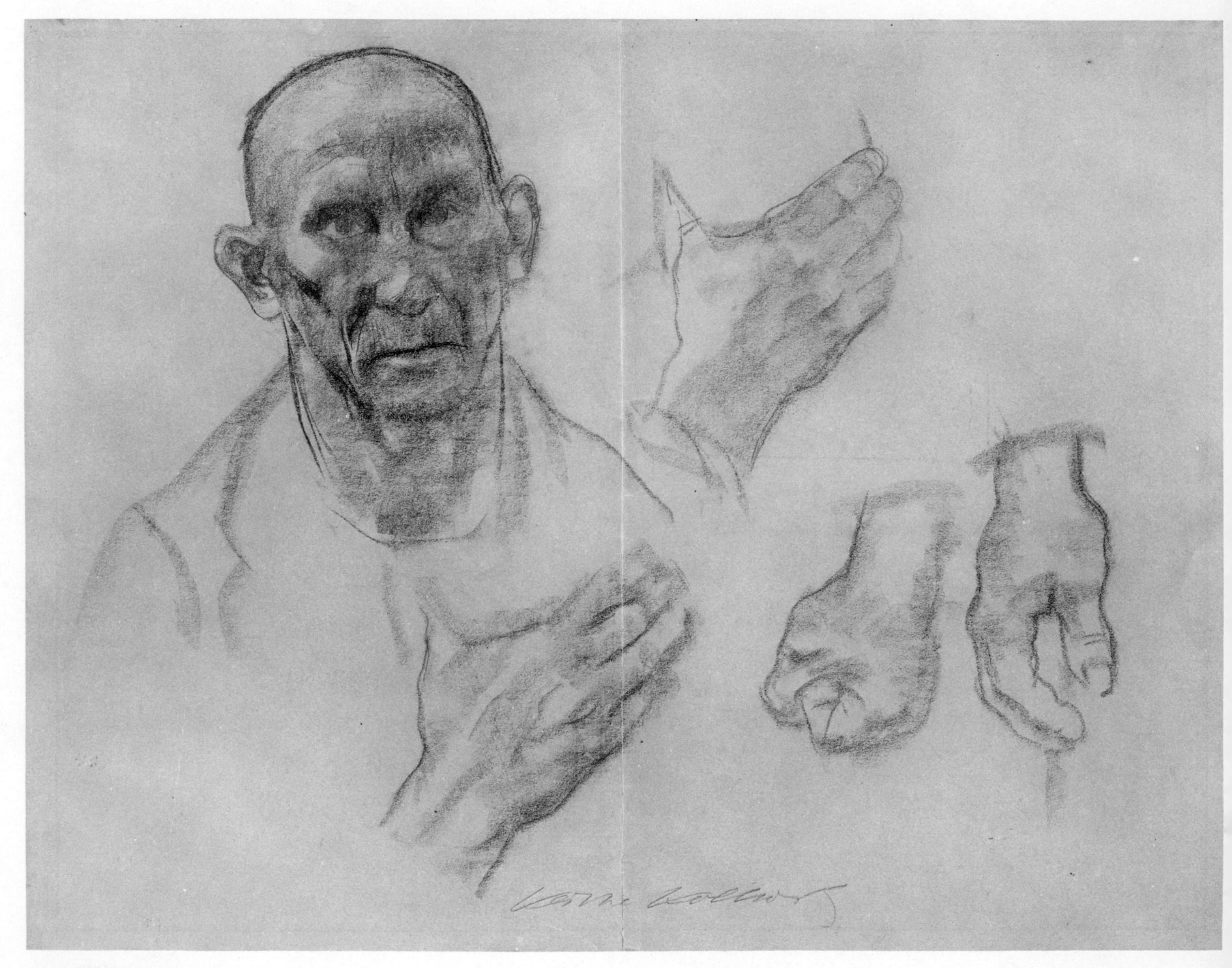

76 Head and Hands of Working Man

77 Woman in Sickbed

78 Mother Leading Two Children

79 Woman Thinking

80 Studies for "In the Waiting Room of the Children's Doctor"

81 Studies for "In the Waiting Room of the Children's Doctor"

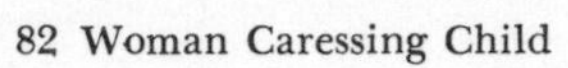

82 Woman Caressing Child

83 Studies of a Sleeping Child

84 Studies of a Baby's Head

85 Double Portrait

86 Death with Woman in Lap

87 The Parents

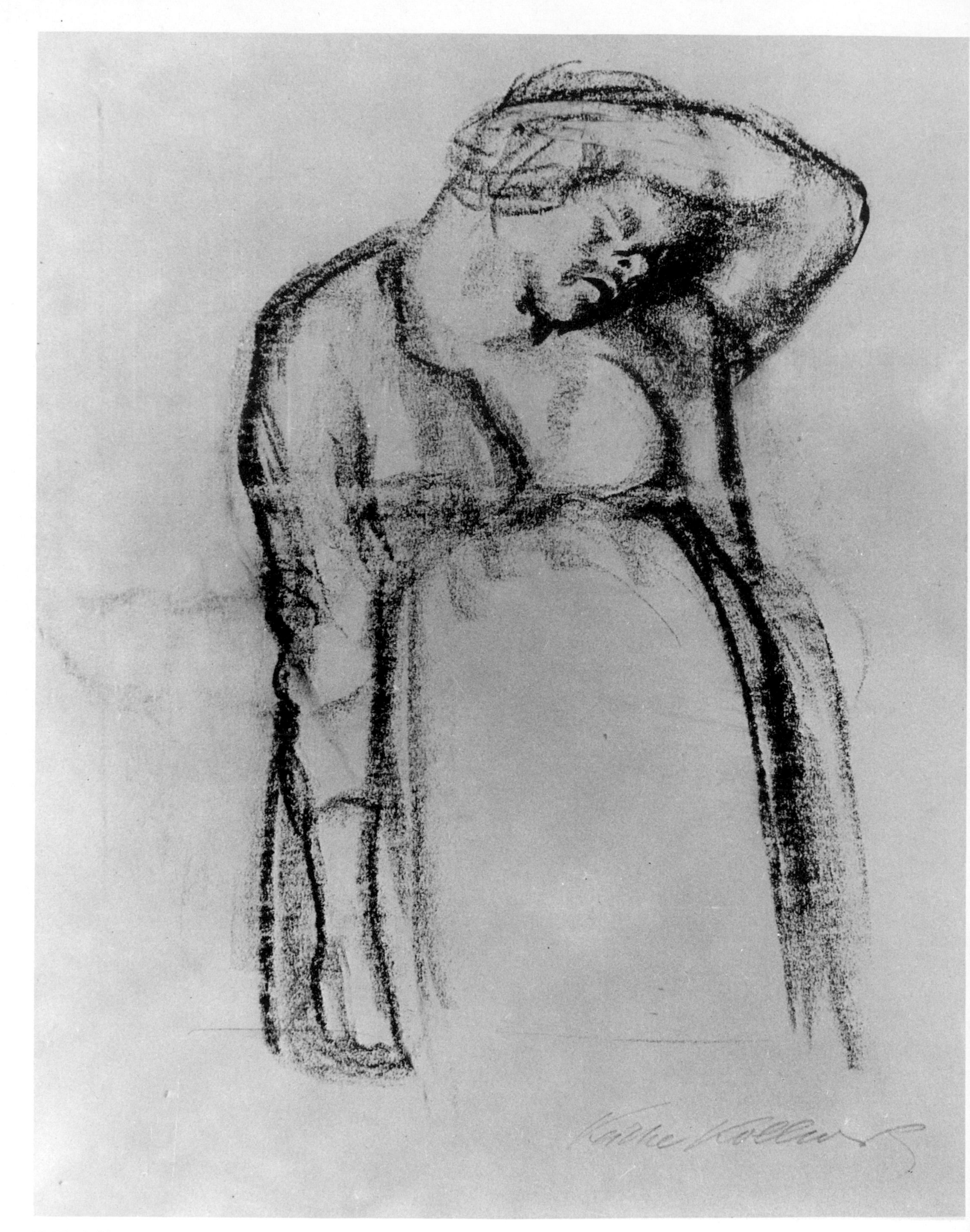

88 The Widow

89 The Volunteers

90 The Widow

91 The Mothers

The People

93 Sketch for "Killed in Action"

1 Killed in Action

95 The Survivors

96 The Survivors

97 Death Reaches for a Woman

98 Death Giving Comfort

99 Sketch for the Poster "Heimarbeit"

100 Woman with Children Going to Their Death

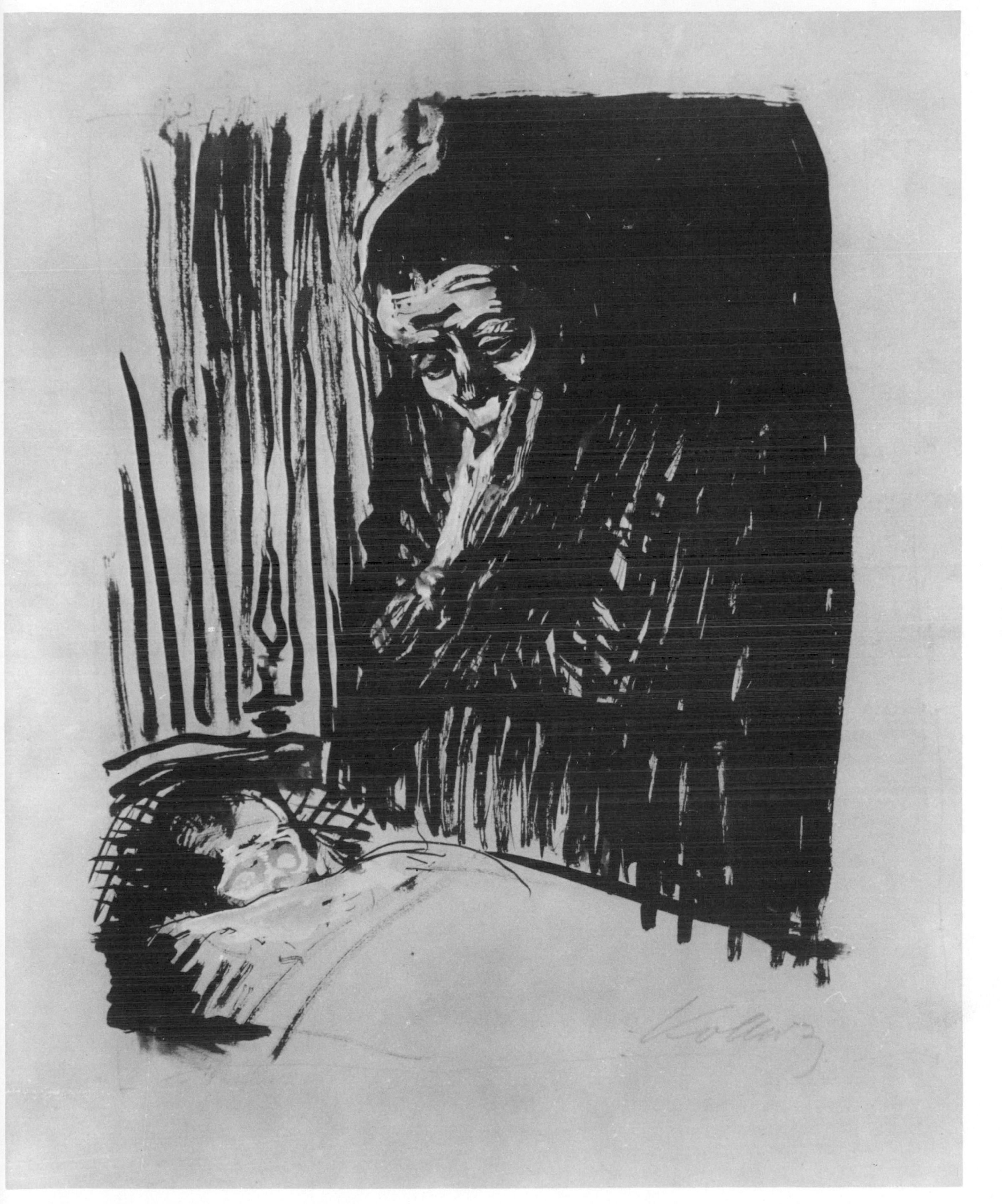

101 Mother and Sick Child

102 Sitting Woman with the Hand of Death

103 Beggars

104 Study for "Germany's Children Starving" (Empty Dishes)

105 Bread!

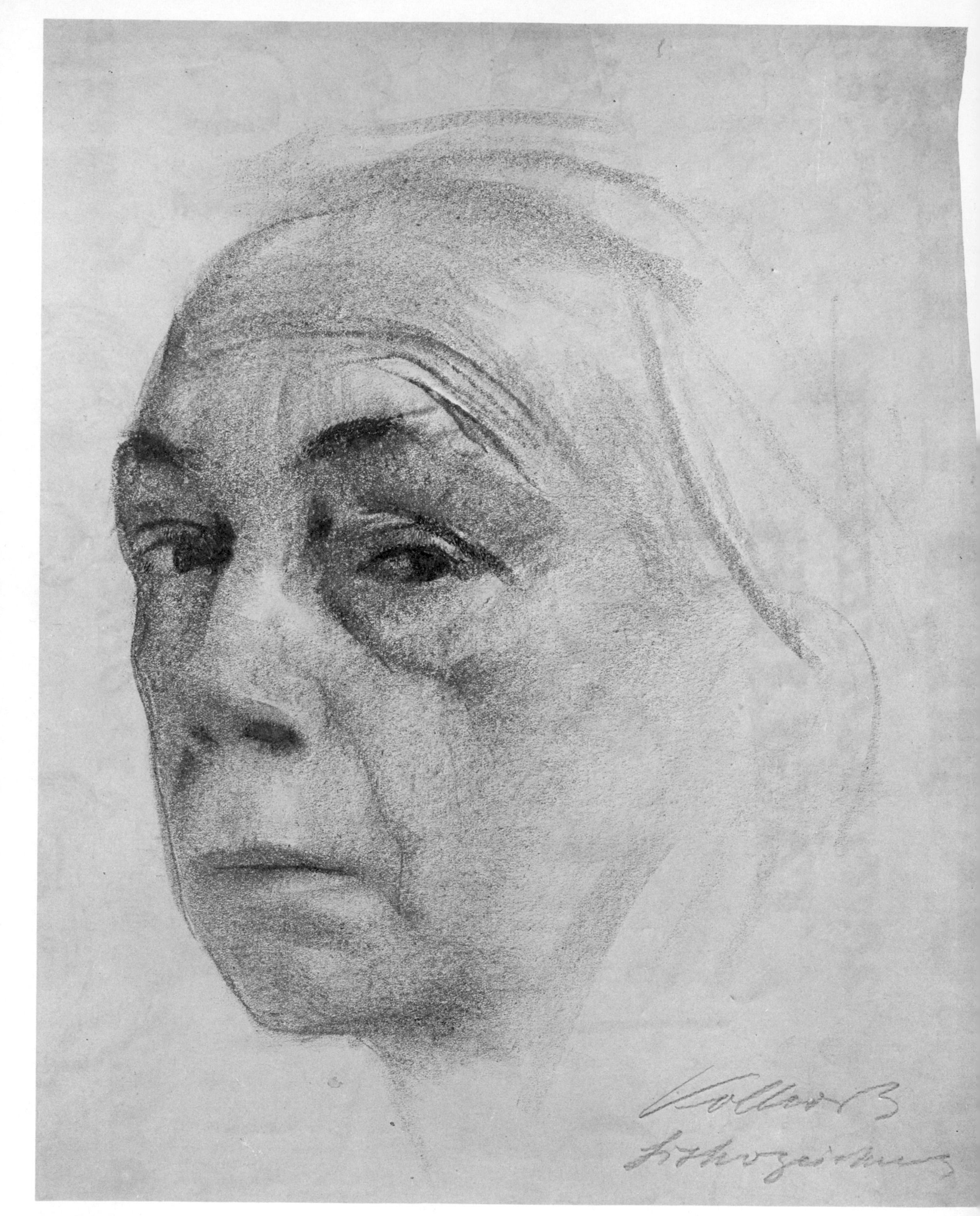

106 Self Portrait

107 Never Again War

108 Unemployed

109 Self Portrait

110 Child's Head (Lotte)

111 Two Children

112 Figure of a Young Girl

113 Prisoners Listening to Music

114 Two Heads

115 Portrait of a Young Man

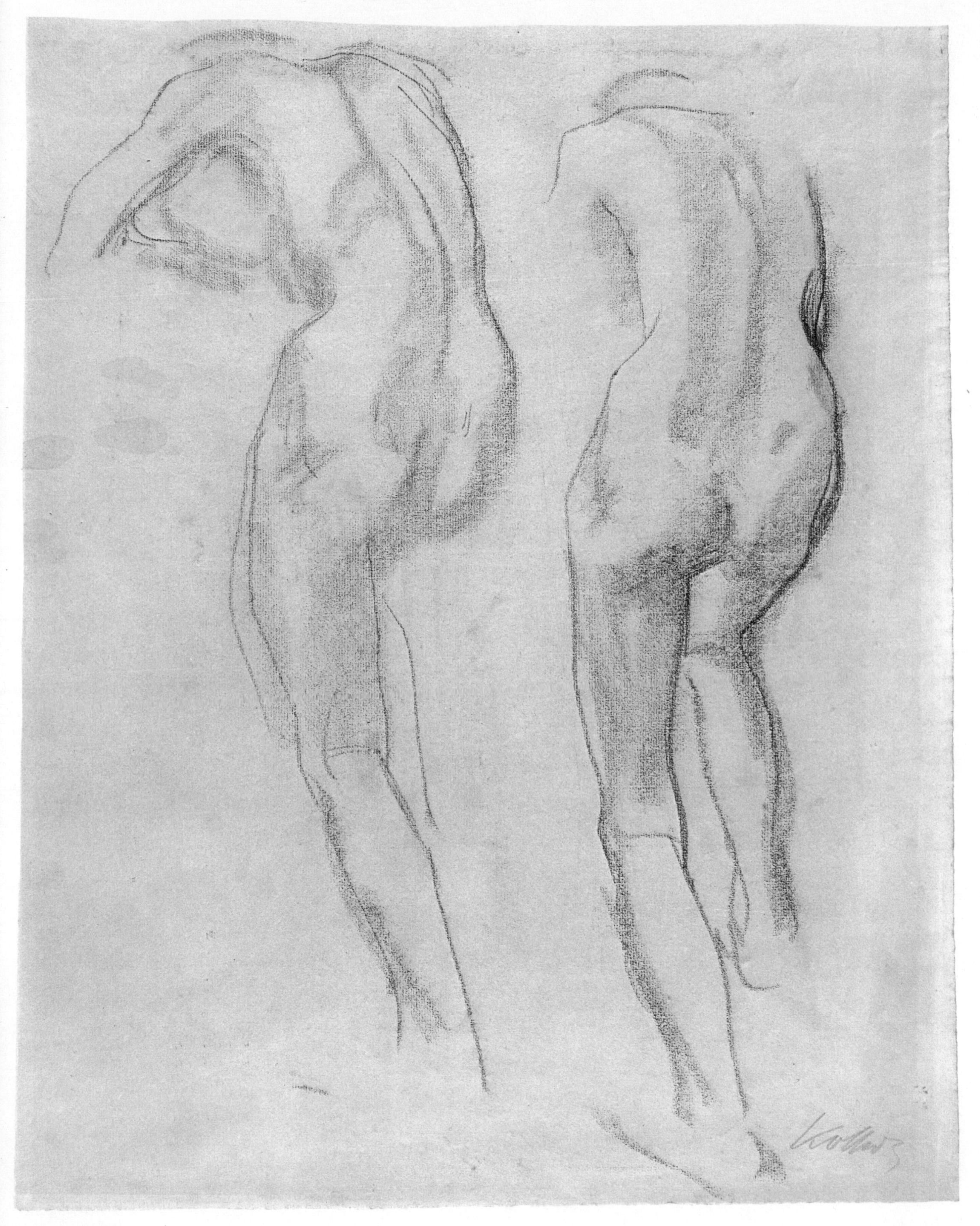

116 Two Nudes

117 Working Woman and Sleeping Boy

118 Maria and Elizabeth

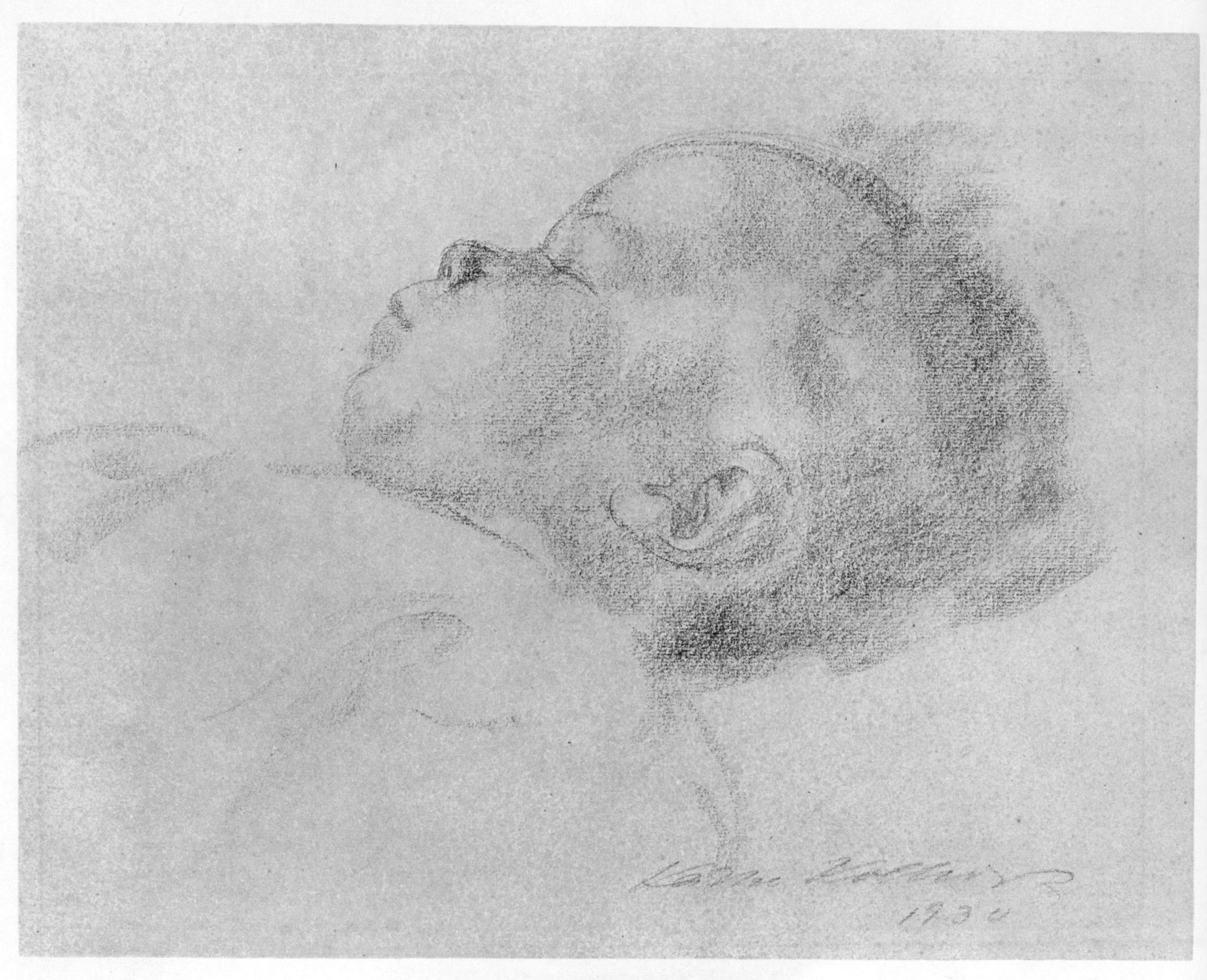

119 Sleeping Boy

120 Sleeping Child

121 Sleeping Child

122 Draft for Roggevelde

Aus dem Nachlaß meiner Mutter Käthe Kollwitz erworben von Herrn Erich Cohn 4. Juni 1950
Hans Kollwitz

123 Draft for Roggevelde

124 Mother and Child

125 Mother with Boy

126 Mother with Children

127 Mother with Children

128 Sitting Woman

129 Two Women

130 Mother and Child

131 Parents and Sick Child

132 Old Couple

133 Mother and Child

134 Alcohol

135 Old Couple

136 Self Portrait

137 Self Portrait

38 Drawing of the Writer Wilhelmine Mohr

139 Sitting Woman

140 Woman Welcoming Death

141 The Hand of Death

142 Mourning Figure: Study for "Death"

143 Fettered Man

144 Mother and Two Children (Standing)

145 Mother and Babies

146 Death Reaches into a Group of Children

147 Self Portrait in Profile to the Right (Lithograph)